D0444376

## My 50 years in baseball, from
## the batter's box to the broadcast booth

# BY RON FAIRLY
### with Steve Springer

**Foreword by Tommy Lasorda**

BACK STORY PUBLISHING, LLC
www.backstorypublishing.com

<u>Fairly at Bat</u>
My 50 years in baseball, from the batter's box to the broadcast booth

*by* Ron Fairly
*with* Steve Springer

Copyright © 2018 by Back Story Publishing, LLC

ISBN: 978-0-9993967-2-8
Library of Congress Control Number: 2017964019

Paperback editions printed in the United States of America. For information on quantity discounts or special editions to be used for educational programs, fundraising, premiums, or sales promotions, please inquire via electronic mail at *admin@BackStoryPublishing.com*, or write to Back Story Publishing, Post Office Box 2580, Rancho Mirage, California 92270 USA.

News media inquiries may be directed to
*newsroom@BackStoryPublishing.com*

Credits
Cover and back cover photographs by Gary Ambrose, copyright © Back Story Publishing LLC

Designer: Stuart Funk
Back Story Publishing Editorial Director: Ellen Alperstein

*www.BackStoryPublishing.com*

## Dedication

To all the guys I played with and against
during my career. We had our good and bad days,
but we all have great memories.

# Foreword

*By Tommy Lasorda*

BASEBALL IS ONE of those games whose aging players remember the people they played with more than the games they played. I remember Ron Fairly well. Never managed him. Wish I had.

When we were younger, Ron and I were both at Vero Beach for spring training. I was a scout at the time, and Ron came to me and asked if I would pitch to him. He needed more work, he said. I said, "Sure." I didn't know he meant PITCH TO HIM EVERY DAY. He did, and I did.

He had this near-perfect batting system. You might get him out, but you wouldn't embarrass him. Swing. Balance. Timing. All perfect. He never looked bad, even when you got him out.

So, we're working at Vero. I'm pitching to him every day. After a couple of weeks, he says to me. "OK, I'm gonna take you out, to downtown Vero." I asked him why. He said he wanted to pay me back for pitching. I said he didn't need to, but he insisted. So, we go to downtown Vero Beach, we go into some stores, and he keeps asking, you want this, you want that? He's holding up sport coats and matching pants, all sorts of nice stuff. I kept telling him that I appreciate the thought, but I'm not going to take anything like that. Then I see this sport shirt. Really fancy one. I said, "Hey, I like that." He buys it.

One day, I found that shirt in my closet. Turned out to be 25 years since he had bought it for me. So, you know what I did?

I sent it back. I bet he still has it.

I remember managing against him in the mid-1970s, mostly when he was with the Cardinals. He got traded to St. Louis just about the time I took over from Walt Alston as the Dodgers manager. He was a tough out, a good right fielder, and first baseman. I remember he had a strong arm, and was accurate with it.

This is a guy who never got the credit he deserved in the majors. He stayed around for 20 years. How many guys can do that? He could hit anybody, and like I said, he never looked bad when he didn't. Ron Fairly played the game right. I always thought he was kind of the model of how a player should be. He was a pro. He represented the game of baseball the right way.

I used to look forward to when he'd come to Dodger Stadium as a broadcaster. He was in Seattle, and also worked for the Angels. I'd invite him to the manager's office, and we'd tell stories and remember stuff. He is a hell of a storyteller. I can't wait to read his book.

*Tommy Lasorda managed the Dodgers from 1977 to 1996. He won two World Series, two awards for Manager of the Year, managed the U.S. baseball team to an Olympic gold medal in 2000 in Sydney, and was inducted into the Baseball Hall of Fame in 1997. He turned 90 in September 2017.*

# Introduction

I N ALL MY YEARS IN BASEBALL — a full 50, which seems unbelievable in retrospect — I never felt like I had a job. It was more like I was going to a playground every day. Except my playground had wide swaths of perfectly manicured, bright green grass, smooth patches of dirt with nary a pebble in sight, brightly colored walls that beckoned to batters, thousands upon thousands of seats, and breathtaking views of towering city skylines or gorgeous, landscaped hillsides.

I played major league baseball for 20 years, then went into the radio and television booth where I spent another three decades. It was a life filled with equal parts drama and humor.

Most kids who dream of becoming a major league ballplayer picture themselves wearing their hometown uniform if they grow up in a big league city. Reality for me was beyond my imagination. Growing up in Long Beach, California, I got to play for one of my hometown universities, USC, was the centerfielder for the Trojans on a team that won the 1958 College World Series, and then, that same year, signed with the new guys in town, the Los Angeles Dodgers, transplanted that season from Brooklyn.

Not only was I blessed to be playing for the team that had largely dominated the National League for more than a decade, but I arrived at a time unlike any other, a transition for the ages. One Dodger dynasty was fading while another was forming.

That first L.A. Dodger roster, back in 1958, contained the names of many holdovers from the Brooklyn glory years, players like Duke

Snider, Pee Wee Reese, Gil Hodges, Carl Furillo, Carl Erskine, Don Newcombe, and Clem Labine.

Though their best days were behind them, they could still play the game. They also could and did pass on the knowledge of the game they had gained over the years, setting the tone for the future. They had a receptive audience because there were legions of talented young ballplayers in the Dodger organization waiting on deck, anxious to secure their own place in the lineup.

Don Drysdale had already established himself by the time the team came west, Sandy Koufax had not yet found himself, while others like me, Maury Wills, Tommy Davis, Willie Davis, Frank Howard, Wes Parker, and Jim Lefebvre, would join the club over the seasons ahead to help create or maintain the next Dodger era of excellence.

GARY AMBROSE © BACK STORY PUBLISHING

We would also learn lessons in both baseball and life from those no longer wearing the Dodger blue, like Jackie Robinson and Roy Campanella, men whose stories and perspective about the franchise and the game kept me spellbound.

Baseball card collectors have no shortage of options for Ron Fairly, who played for 20 years.

Along the way, I also interacted with Hall of Famers like Ted Williams, Hank Aaron, Willie Mays, and Bob Gibson, and their stories are also in this book.

In my half-century, I had hundreds of teammates and colleagues, roommates and travel companions, who made the journey so enjoyable. Every player, whether on winning or losing teams, can look back in retirement at memorable games in which they participated, but it was what we did before and after it was time to play ball that I miss the most. You can't put 35 or 40 guys together for seven or eight months a year, travel around the country, spend more time with each other than with their families, and not generate lasting memories. During my playing days, my teammates and I probably spent more time away from our hotel rooms than players do today. We didn't have computers and video equipment to entertain us.

We did have one simple rule: Do not criticize a player's ability. Everything else was fair game as long as it was in jest. We could tease a teammate about his clothes, have fun with him for something dumb that he said, or something ridiculous that he did.

Here are a few examples of incidents that elicited no sympathy from teammates, and a few words of wisdom that did.

- Nolan Ryan, Hall of Fame pitcher for the Angels and three other teams, was bitten by a coyote.
- Brian Anderson, a pitcher for the Angels and three other clubs, burned himself ironing a shirt *while wearing it.*
- Steve Sparks, a pitcher for the Angels and four other teams, hurt his shoulder trying to rip a phone book in half.
- Dave Goltz, pitcher for the Angels (notice a pattern?), Dodgers, and Twins, cut the middle finger of his pitching hand getting tissue from a toilet-paper dispenser.
- Glenallen Hill, outfielder for the Angels and six other clubs, while having a nightmare about spiders, fell down a flight of stairs.
- Richie Sexson, first baseman/outfielder for five teams, hurt his neck putting on his baseball cap.
- Hall of Fame Manager Whitey Herzog disliked extra-inning games in spring training because he had other priorities. "I don't need 12 or 13 innings to evaluate a player," he said. "My pitching coach needs to make sure we have a cocktail pitcher in the bullpen — if the game goes into extra innings, I want a pitcher who can give up a run or two so we can all go and have a cocktail."

Not all the characters in baseball have been players. They include announcers, clubhouse men, scouts, traveling secretaries, and, yes, even the grounds crew. In 1965, the Dodgers, after beating the Twins in the World

Series, voted to give their grounds crew a full winners' share of the players' pool money generated by World Series ticket sales. The money was to be divided equally among the four-man crew. A check was given to the head groundskeeper, but, instead of distributing the money, he kept it all and skipped town.

My years in uniform generated enough stories to fill a book, and many people, having heard me tell some of those stories on the air as a broadcaster, said I should indeed put them in a book.

So here we are. I have included stories about the special players and unforgettable characters who have crossed my path, the fantastic games and wild times I've been fortunate enough to be a part of, the moments heralded in headlines, and those that will never be found in a box score.

You will read about the pitcher, the girl, and the violinist; the only pitcher ever to get the hook from his manager in the middle of batting practice; the horse that ran for the stables instead of the finish line with stacks of Dodgers money riding on him; and the Dodger who had to talk fans out of murdering an opponent.

Hope you enjoy my trip down memory lane, and maybe get a laugh or two.

— Ron Fairly

# *1*

## Catching History

WHEN I FIRST SAW the shiny white baseball soaring across the deep blue sky, headed in my direction, it seemed to be beyond my grasp. Going back all the way to the right-field fence in front of the visiting team's bullpen at Dodger Stadium, I still figured the ball was more likely to land over the fence in a reliever's glove rather than in my own. Or maybe it would carom into the hands of one of the fans in the right-field seats who would have been more than willing to exchange his beer cup for a priceless souvenir.

It was a pivotal moment for me, for the Dodgers, for baseball history. We were facing the New York Yankees in the 1963 World Series.

No surprise. There had been 16 World Series since 1947. The Yankees had been in 13 of them, winning 10, including five in a row from 1949 to 1953. It was an unbelievable stretch of dominance.

It had been six years since the Brooklyn Dodgers had departed their ancestral home, the New York Giants joining them in a move to the West Coast. There was shock, sadness, and outrage at the time, but the Yankees now had an opportunity to complete a double whammy against the teams that had deserted the Big Apple.

After beating the Cincinnati Reds in the 1961 World Series, the Yankees had exacted some revenge for their city by defeating the San Francisco Giants in the '62 World Series. Beating us would be just as sweet. And nothing new. The Yankees had beaten the Dodgers in six of their previous seven World Series confrontations, losing only in 1955, when Brooklyn won its only world championship.

Playing in Yankee Stadium can be tough on any visiting team any time of the year. It's the holy grail of baseball. It's where Babe Ruth, Lou Gehrig, Joe DiMaggio, and other Yankee greats set records and established a level of team excellence that set them apart from all others. Considering the size of the stadium, the dimensions, the pinstripe uniforms, and the history, it can be an overwhelming experience. Just the idea that you're standing in the batter's box where Ruth and Gehrig stood makes the experience special.

The first thing I do when I step onto the Yankee Stadium field is to go to Monument Park beyond the outfield where there are statues, plaques, and retired numbers honoring the greatest to ever wear the pinstripes.

After I soaked all this in at the start of the 1963 World Series, I thought, How much are we going to get beat by?

We knew we had a good team, but then again, we were playing the Yankees.

They had a lot more power in their lineup than we did. The difference was glaring. New York hit 188 home runs in 1963, while we had knocked only 110 balls out of the park. They had been called the Bronx Bombers for many years and, with a power-laden roster led by Mickey Mantle and Roger Maris, they were very confident in their ability to win by maintaining their traditional philosophy of relying on the long ball as the No. 1 weapon in their arsenal.

How were we going to stop these guys from scoring a dozen runs a game? What we wanted to do was keep the ball in the park whenever possible, and stop the guys who hit in front of the power hitters from getting on base, so if they did hit a home run, it would be a solo shot rather than a two- or three-run homer. Stay away from the big inning.

We, in contrast, won with pitching, defense, and speed, scratching out a few more runs than the opposition. Our manager, Walter Alston, said many times, "Give me a team with a bunch of .270 to .280 hitters that don't strike out much, and I'll beat you more times than you beat me."

As it turned out, thanks to our superlative pitching, we actually edged them in home runs in the series, 3-2. Frank Howard, Bill Skowron, and Johnny Roseboro homered for us, Mantle, and Tom Tresh for them.

In Game 1, Sandy Koufax was dominating, leading us to a 5-2 victory. He allowed two runs and six hits in a complete-game performance, striking out a then-World Series record 15, including the first five hitters he faced.

At times, his fastball was just unhittable. Yankee second baseman Bobby Richardson was a good high-fastball hitter. Koufax struck him out three times, all on high fastballs. I don't think Richardson had seen a guy quite like that. And, it was the same thing with a lot of their other hitters. They saw a fastball they were not familiar with.

The last batter of the game was Harry Bright, who came in as a pinch hitter. He had no chance. There were shadows around home plate when he walked up there cold off the bench in the latter part of the afternoon. So not only did Bright have to try to catch up to a fastball that had blown away so many of his teammates, but he had to do so at a time when it was tough to pick the ball up as it came out of Koufax's hand. It was a mismatch, Bright becoming strikeout No. 15.

In Game 2, our starter was left-hander Johnny Podres. If a game was not crucial, there was no telling what Johnny was going to do or where he had been the night before. You never knew what you were going to get.

In the closing days of the 1963 regular season, we had clinched the pennant, so we had time to organize our pitching staff heading into the World Series. Alston decided to make our next-to-last game of the regular season a tuneup outing for Podres. He wanted his left-hander to throw at least five innings to get ready for Game 2 of the World Series.

Facing the Philadelphia Phillies, Podres got clobbered. In $1^{2}/_3$ innings, he gave up eight runs on 12 hits.

Out to the mound went Alston.

"How do you feel?" he asked his pitcher.

"For God's sakes, get me out of here before I get somebody killed," said Johnny. "This is enough of the tuneup shit."

He handed Alston the ball. The skipper hadn't asked for it, but Johnny gave it to him nonetheless.

We had two great pitchers in Koufax and Don Drysdale. But if a season was on the line, I just might start Podres over either of those two guys because, in that situation, you could feel confident Johnny would be fantastic. He could give our team seven or eight strong innings and keep us in a ballgame. If we could score a couple of runs for him, that would be enough.

Podres' greatest game was in Yankee Stadium in the 1955 World Series. He pitched a complete-game shutout in Game 7, giving the Dodgers a 2-0 victory and the only World Series triumph they would attain in their days in Brooklyn.

In Game 2 of the '63 World Series, Podres went 8⅓ innings, allowing six hits and a run. Reliever Ron Perranoski came in to finish up a 4-1 victory.

For Game 3, the scene shifted to Dodger Stadium. The Dodgers scored in the first inning when Jim Gilliam walked, advanced to second on a wild pitch, and scored on a Tommy Davis single.

When the inning was over, I jokingly told Drysdale, our starting pitcher, "There's your lead. Hold on to it."

As the game wore on, it became obvious that was just what Don was going to have to do, and he was up to the challenge. He faced only 33 batters, allowed just three hits, struck out nine, and walked one (an intentional walk to Clete Boyer to get to the pitcher, Jim Bouton, with the bases loaded in the second inning). Drysdale struck Bouton out and went on to retire 18 of the last 21 batters he faced.

In the sixth inning, Mantle struck out. I was trotting in from right field and Mickey was going out to center. As we passed, he said, "Ron, tell Drysdale to lighten up on me. He's making me look bad."

Still, as we went into the ninth inning, I was scared as hell because the Yankees were sending up Tresh, Mantle, and Joe Pepitone, their No. 3, 4, and 5 hitters. Tresh struck out and Mantle grounded to first.

One more to go.

Pepitone had hit 27 home runs in the regular season. If he could get one more here, it might be a very different series. He was a good low-fastball hitter, and Don had a good sinking fastball (actually, truth be told, it was a very good spitter), so it was strength against strength.

On his second pitch, Drysdale threw Pepitone a change-up that he connected on, hitting that towering fly ball to right.

Although I initially thought from the trajectory that it was headed over the fence, I raced back, feeling the dirt of the warning track on my cleats. As I picked up the flight of the ball, I could feel a slight breeze blowing from the right I kept muttering to myself, "Get him wind, get him!"

I sneaked a glance at the fence and the Yankee pitchers behind it, rooting the ball on. I still had a little more room, so I backed up a few more feet.

Finally, much to my relief, I could tell the ball was going to come down just short of the fence. It was playable. If I could catch it, we would win and go up three games to none with Koufax, one of the best pitchers in baseball history at the peak of his career, ready to take the mound in Game 4.

But I realized I had one last problem. The ball had drifted directly into the sun, always a hazard on cloudless afternoons at Dodger Stadium. I flipped my sunglasses down, but they were too dark. I couldn't see the ball very well. So, I flipped the glasses back up and used my glove to shade my eyes.

Down came the ball, finally settling into my glove. Elation swept over me. We had won, 1-0.

In the clubhouse afterward, a beaming Drysdale told me, "I thought you were kidding when you said, 'There's your lead. Hold on to it.'"

*I* thought I was kidding. But it turned out to be one of the best performances of Drysdale's Hall of Fame career.

In Game 4, the Yankees found themselves right back in the line of fire, Koufax being as tough to hit as he had been in Game 1.

Howard hit a solo home run in the fifth inning, but Mantle matched that with a solo homer of his own in the seventh. Then, in the bottom of that inning, Gilliam hit a high bouncer to third. Boyer fielded it and threw to first, but Pepitone lost the ball in the largely white-shirted crowd. It bounced off his arm, ricocheted off the railing, and rolled down the right-field line. By the time the Yankees recovered, Gilliam was sliding safely into third. Willie Davis hit a sacrifice fly to drive him in.

That gave us a 2-1 lead, and, with Koufax on the mound again pitching a masterful complete game, that's the way it ended.

It was an historic victory for us, the only World Series sweep in Dodger history, and only the second time the Yankees had been swept in the World Series, a feat first accomplished by the Giants in 1922.

What was amazing to me was that we had done this using a total of only 13 players in the four games. There were four pitchers, Koufax,

Drysdale, and Podres as the starters, with Perranoski pitching in relief in Game 2. The starting lineup never changed with the exception of Game 3, when I replaced Skowron. Alston also brought me in to replace Howard in right field for defensive purposes in the latter stages of the other three games. But that was it. Nobody else came off the bench.

Skowron, a right-handed hitter, hit left-handers well, and he was very comfortable in Yankee Stadium, where he had played for the previous nine years. That's why he started the three games in which we faced left-handers. During the season, he had hit only .203 for us with four home runs and 19 RBIs. Alston played a hunch by starting him in the World Series and Skowron responded by doing a hell of a job. He hit .385 with a home run and three RBIs. That was a smart move by Alston.

**Doused with Champagne, Ron Fairly celebrates the Dodgers' World Series championship in 1963.**

© (1963) ASSOCIATED PRESS

In the middle of the wild clubhouse celebration, the booze spraying everywhere, I think each of us paused at some point to soak in the magnitude of what had just happened. We had beaten our old tormentors, the most successful franchise in baseball history, in the World Series in four straight.

It was the greatest moment in Dodger history.

# 2

## A Solid Foundation

I GUESS I WAS DESTINED to wind up playing for the Dodgers with the Los Angeles Memorial Coliseum becoming my first major-league home field. Baseball was in my DNA. And seeing the Coliseum was one of my earliest memories.

My dad, Carl Chester Fairly, was a professional baseball player, an infielder who spent 11 years in the minors.

I'd like to think I inspired him because he had a very good season in 1938, the year I was born in Macon, Georgia. Playing at the Class B level for the Macon Peaches of the South Atlantic League, Dad hit .302 with a .406 slugging percentage and 34 doubles in a season that concluded with a league championship for the Peaches.

I still have one of his contracts from the mid-1930s. Paid $85 a month, Dad sent $50 to Mom and lived on the remaining $35. He rented a place for $25 a month, and that included two meals a day, so that left him with a whopping $10 for himself.

We moved to Southern California three months after I was born. It remained home for me, my mother, Marjorie Van Loan, and my brother, Rusty (who was 5½ years older than me), while my dad moved from team to team. We lived first in Boyle Heights, then in a place near the Coliseum. As a young kid, I was in awe of that big saucer, never imaging I would one day pound its walls and seats with baseballs.

Of course, in those days, no one could have imagined baseball would be played in a stadium known for the Olympics and football.

Among the favorite memories of my childhood were the occasional,

In the early 1930s, Ron's father, Carl Chester Fairly, represented Houghton Park in Long Beach, California, where some guy named Babe Ruth was hanging around, representing the Yankees of New York.

unannounced visits of my grandfather, Paul Van Loan. He was a musical director who worked for Sonja Henie, the Norwegian Olympic figure skating champion who went on to become a very successful entertainer and movie star.

Armed with bags of groceries and accompanied by a few of his buddies, my grandfather would poke his head through our front door and yell out to my mother, "Hey, Marjorie, we're hungry. How about fixing us some dinner."

The groceries he had brought with him were enough for a week's worth of dinners. Because we were living paycheck to paycheck, it was like manna from heaven.

After we had eaten, a poker game would break out, Grandpa's hearty laugh echoing through the house.

One day, my parents bought a house, sight unseen, in North Long

Beach. It cost $5,000 with mortgage payments of $50 a month.

It was a great neighborhood in which to grow up. I don't know if we even had a front-door key, but I know we never locked that door.

When the baseball season ended each year, Dad would come home and find work to get us through the winter months financially before going back to baseball in the spring. He worked as a welder in the Long Beach ship yards and later as a dispatcher and manager for a chain of drug stores.

On Sundays in the offseason, we would drive to South Pasadena where Dad played baseball for the Rosabell Plumbers in a semi-pro league. The Plumbers had several major leaguers on the team who wanted to stay

in shape. The team played a doubleheader every week. For the two games, Dad got $20.

My brother and I had our own payment plan. We ran after foul balls and brought them back so they could be used again. For our effort, we were each given a hot dog and a Coke between games. One

FAIRLY FAMILY

Carl Fairly demonstrates proper batting technique to his left-handed son, Ron, in the 1940s.

Sunday, Rusty and I brought back just about every foul ball hit. Our reward: two hot dogs each.

When I was 10, I got a weekend job at a sporting goods store owned by a man named Charlie Brown, dusting, sweeping floors, running errands, and whatever else a young kid could do. I used the money for my first baseball glove.

With the help of the city of Long Beach, Brown formed the Kid Baseball Association, one of the first organized leagues for kids in Southern California. I played for the PDQ (sponsored by Pretty Darn Quick gasoline) Pelicans, one of the four teams in the league.

About that same time, I also started playing basketball at the downtown Long Beach YMCA for a coach named George "Shorty" Kellogg. His focus was on the importance of sportsmanship and good character.

He had a saying that I've never forgotten: "Play hard and give your best effort," he would tell us, "and if you lose, lose only the game and not the respect of your opponents."

We need more Shorty Kelloggs in the world.

As I approached my teens, I moved up to a league for older kids. All the teams had the names of their sponsors on the back of their uniforms, names like Al's Auto Body Parts, Danny's Liquor Store, and Bill's Barber Shop. My sponsor was Miriam's Beauty Bar. I hated that jersey because every time I came up to the plate, I heard, "Here comes Miriam's Beauty Bar." I still hate that jersey.

FAIRLY FAMILY

This glove was active during Ron's high-school career.

With his own baseball career over, Dad loved to work with the local kids. Working for a baseball recreational program developed by the city, Dad entered a team of kids in a city softball league for players ages 17 to 20. Though the kids that played for him were mostly 15- to 17-year-olds, he talked league officials into letting them play.

Unfortunately, those kids acted their age. Most of the time if they didn't win, they got into fights.

One hot summer day, all the guys were at our house getting ready for a game that afternoon. We heard the trademark musical sound of the Good Humor ice cream truck as it came down the street and stopped right in front of our house.

After the neighbors had bought some ice cream, the Good Humor man was ready to move on, but he couldn't start his truck.

He asked if the team would give him a push.

In the 1950s, Ron was the batboy for the American Legion Post 27 team at Recreation Park in Long Beach. His father, Carl, far right, was a coach.

Well, they pushed all right, the truck moving slowly down the street. But while some actually pushed, others opened the back of the truck and stole several large boxes of ice cream. They gave the truck a big, final push. It started, and the Good Humor man went merrily down the street, jingling all the way.

It was a month before that truck came down our street again.

The players ate a lot of the ice cream, put the rest in our refrigerator, and came by the next few days to finish off the spoils of their ice cream caper.

When my mom found out what had happened, she raised hell with the players and made them put money into a jar every week until there was enough to pay the Good Humor man back.

Tony Mabry was the biggest, toughest kid on my dad's team. He was also a good athlete, but his attitude often got in the way.

Tony's father had a drinking problem, and abused him. No wonder he got into a lot of fights at school.

Because he lived only a couple blocks from us, it was easier to hang around our home than to deal with his own father.

Mom would bake cookies for him or occasionally invite him for dinner. Dad, Rusty, Tony, and I would sit around the table talking baseball. Both my parents would urge Tony to try harder in school.

We never had a problem with him at our house. Tony would look for ways to help my mom with the household chores.

But once he was out of our house, the old Tony would surface. Before one night game, he addressed his teammates, telling them, "We're going to win the game, and the fight afterward, too."

Then Dad reminded the whole squad that officials had allowed their team to join the league only if they conducted themselves properly and demonstrated good sportsmanship. "I gave my word," Dad said, "that we would honor those expectations and I will be personally responsible for each player on this team."

They won the game that night, and afterward there was no fight.

The next day, Dad named Tony team captain. After that, if anyone got out of line, Tony kicked that player's ass.

My dad gave those kids a sense of direction. He taught them the fundamentals of baseball and the rules of the game. Teaching them sportsmanship took a little longer, but they got there.

Dad always wanted to know how they were doing in school. "The first person you don't want to cheat is yourself," Dad would tell them. "If you do, you'll cheat the team as well. Take advantage of what's available to you at school. You can't play forever."

The season ended. Dad's team won the city championship. Two of the other team coaches wanted Dad's squad kicked out of the league for being too young. My dad suggested that their teams might have more success in the 11- to 14-year-old division.

Looking for a new challenge, my dad moved up from the softball league to coach the American Legion Post 27 baseball squad, made up primarily of kids from Long Beach Poly High School. It was known as a football school with quite a few of its players going on to the NFL, but Dad found some baseball talent as well.

My brother Rusty played some baseball, but football became his sport. At the University of Denver, he played for Coach Bob Blackman. Rusty's biggest year in football was 1954, when the Denver Pioneers were 9-1, and became champions of the Skyline Conference for the third time in their history. Rusty was a quarterback and receiver on offense, a cornerback on defense, and a punter and placekicker on special teams.

First in the nation that season in interceptions, my brother led the Skyline All-Stars to victory in the 1955 New Year's Day Salad Bowl in Phoenix, and was named Most Valuable Player of the game, after having been named honorable mention All-America by the Associated Press. Nicknamed The Mad Magician, my brother had previously been voted All-Skyline Conference in 1953 and 1954.

Rusty played one season in the Canadian Football League, but his pro career was cut short due to a knee injury. He followed my father into coaching, first for the University of Denver and then, in 1961, at Santa Barbara City College, where he coached both football and baseball during his quarter-century on that campus.

Rusty was inducted into the Santa Barbara Athletic Round Table Hall of Fame, and into the Hall of Fame at both the University of Denver and Long Beach City College.

When he left sports, he found a second career in politics, serving three terms on the Santa Barbara City Council.

I am very proud of my brother and the lives he touched.

Whatever he and I accomplished in life, we owe to Dad and Mom. They taught us the values we always carried with us.

So, although Dad was serious about baseball, and winning was important to him, because it's how he had made a living, when we were grade-school kids, the most important thing to him was that we learned to be good teammates, and to have fun. Too many parents put pressure on their kids to win, and they miss the bigger picture. Very few kids become professional ballplayers, but every kid can have fun just learning to appreciate a sport.

Because Dad was on the road playing baseball in our early years and then worked a lot at night when he retired from the game, he often missed the games we played as kids and then teenagers.

When he got home, he had five questions for us, in this order:

1.  Did you play? If we said yes, he went on.
2.  Did you have any fun?
3.  What did you do to have fun?
4.  Did you get any hits, and if so, where did you hit them?
5.  Were any balls hit to you, and if so, were there base runners? What did you do with the ball when you caught it?
6.  Did you win?

As far as Mom was concerned, if I didn't get good grades, I wouldn't be allowed to play sports. I got the message. The one thing I never wanted to hear from Mom or Dad was, "You disappointed me."

Dad, Mom, and Rusty are all gone now, but I still have a trophy to remind me of those early years.

Rusty and I gave it to Dad one Christmas with this inscription:

TO A PLAYER'S COACH
TO A MAN'S MAN
AND
TO OUR DAD,
THE GREATEST COACH EVER
— *RUSTY AND RON*

# 3

## Baseball 101
## With Professor Dedeaux

WHEN I ENTERED Long Beach Jordan High School, I realized that all those years of watching Dad play, seeing him interact as a coach with his players, and listening to his advice had provided me with a launching pad for my own career.

With a firm grasp of fundamentals and an understanding of the philosophy of the game, I excelled, hitting .514 as a senior in 1956. I was named CIF co-player of the year, sharing the honor with Mike McCormick of Mark Keppel High in Alhambra, a left-handed pitcher who went on to a 16-year career in the majors, and won a Cy Young Award in 1967.

The CIF award resulted in an invitation for both Mike and me to play in the 1956 Hearst Sandlot Classic at the Polo Grounds in New York, the home field of the Giants back then. The game was a big deal in those days for the participants, a chance for young players to perform on a national stage and, they hoped, attract the attention of college recruiters and major league scouts.

Mike and I were taken to New York by John B. Old, a columnist for the Los Angeles Herald-Examiner, a Hearst newspaper.

It was a big thrill to play, at the age of 18, at the Polo Grounds, but I was equally excited when I learned batting practice would be held across town at Yankee Stadium, the most famous ballpark in America. I actually hit one into the seats that day. I felt like I had just won a game.

Not only did Mr. Old arrange for us to see a game there as well,

Yankees against the Boston Red Sox, but he also got us on the field for the two teams' batting practice.

And I got to meet the Yankees legendary manager, Casey Stengel.

"Are you a hitter?" Casey asked when I stepped down into the Yankee dugout.

"Yeah, I think so," I said.

"Go up and watch that guy who is in the batting cage now," Casey said. "He's very good. If anybody asks you what you are doing there, tell them I sent you."

I didn't know who was hitting. All I saw was No. 9 on his back. When I saw his face, I was in awe. It was Ted Williams. He put on a show while I was standing there, crushing ball after ball.

When I came back to the dugout, Casey said, "If you can do what he can do, you're going to be pretty good."

No kidding.

When I got back home, I was faced with a decision about my future. I wanted to go to college and I wasn't going to have to worry about finding one that would accept me. They found me.

I had an offer to go to Stanford and play for Dutch Fehring, who had just completed his first season as the college's baseball coach, but would go on to win 290 games in 12 years on the job, then a school record. He would also take Stanford to the College World Series in 1967.

I had an even better offer in my own backyard, a scholarship at UCLA — a basketball scholarship offered by the head coach, a man named John Wooden.

I had averaged 18 points a game in my last year at Jordan, but I wanted to focus on baseball in college.

Somebody at UCLA suggested I talk to Art Reichle, the baseball coach, and that maybe I could play both sports there.

Reichle was a nice enough man, but, a quarter-century before Jackie Robinson Stadium opened, there was nothing nice about the UCLA campus baseball field. It was wide open with no outfield fences at a reasonable distance. Center field stretched out to 500 feet from home plate. The field was in raggedy shape and part of the surrounding structure was torn open. I was less than impressed.

When I came home, I didn't have to explain to my dad how the visit went. He could tell from the look on my face.

He shrugged and said, "Why don't you go talk to Rod Dedeaux?" I learned that my dad, who seemed to know everybody in baseball, knew Rod, the USC baseball coach, very well.

When I met Rod, I instantly liked him. Who didn't like Rod Dedeaux, for goodness sakes? While Reichle had been friendly, he couldn't match Rod in terms of his personality and enthusiasm. Also, USC had a better baseball team and overall program than UCLA.

But ultimately, the determining factor was the ballpark. I went out to Bovard Field where the Trojans played their games and the first thing I saw was a fence, the right-field fence. Down the line, it was just 318 feet from home plate, a short porch that would be ideal for a left-handed hitter like me. It was only 344 to right center. And, as I soon learned, there was usually a little afternoon breeze blowing in from left field that would help the ball carry a little bit more toward that fence in right. It would be a lot better than playing at UCLA in a ballpark where it seemed like there was no end to the field.

I learned after I started playing for USC that the area beyond the right-field fence, well beyond it, had been the landing spot for one of the most historic home runs ever hit out of any ballpark anywhere.

Among Rod's friends was Casey Stengel, who lived nearby in Glendale. It was a connection that went back to 1935, when Rod made his only appearance in the major leagues, playing in two games for a Brooklyn Dodgers team managed by Casey. A back injury ended Rod's dreams of a big league career, but the relationship with Stengel endured.

Six years before I came to USC, the Yankees, holding spring training in Arizona, were playing a series of exhibition games on the West Coast.

Casey and Rod agreed to play one of those games at Bovard Field, the two-time defending world champions against a college team. Rod thought it would be a great experience for his players.

The game was played on March 26, 1951, and those who were there never forgot it. That's because of a spectacular performance by a 19-year-old rookie by the name of Mickey Mantle, who had yet to play in his first regular-season game. Batting left-handed in the first inning, Mantle hit a pitch from Tom Lovrich, a 6-foot-5-inch right-hander in his junior year, over the right-field fence, but that was only the beginning of its journey.

Beyond the fence was a practice football field, 50 yards wide and perpendicular to the diamond with another fence on its far side. There were 30 feet of sideline area on each side of the field.

Mantle's blast cleared the fence in right center at the 344-foot mark and continued on an upward arc over the 30-foot sideline.

At that point, myth clouds reality. According to one account, the ball soared over the entire width of the field before bouncing on the other sideline and then over the far fence. That would have meant that the ball would have traveled approximately 656 feet, the longest home run in baseball history.

In a Los Angeles Times story, a few members of the football team who were practicing at the time, said that the ball landed in the middle of their field and rolled into their huddle. That would make the length of the homer closer to 550 to 600 feet.

Incredibly, Mantle wasn't done that day. In the same game, swinging right-handed, he hit a home run that cleared the left-field wall, flew over the street, carried over two houses across that street, and landed on the roof of a third house. Although that blast wasn't officially measured, it was estimated to have traveled well over 500 feet, perhaps approaching 600.

In his five at-bats that day, he had a single, triple, the two home runs, and seven RBIs as the Yankees won, 15-1.

Rod called it, "The greatest show in history."

Mantle went on to set the official record for the longest home run in major league history. He hit it in 1953 off Washington Senators pitcher Chuck Stobbs in Washington's Griffith Stadium, the ball traveling 565 feet.

I wasn't dreaming about setting home run distance records when I first put on a Trojan uniform. I just wanted to play for the varsity. But that wasn't possible in my first year because freshmen were not allowed to play at the varsity level. It was tough to wait a full year, but it was worth it when I got to spend my sophomore season on Rod's squad.

He was an easy coach to play for as long as you concentrated on the fundamentals of the game and understood the situation on the field at all times. Always know where to throw the ball and why, he'd say. In that way, he was just like my dad. The coaching I got from Rod reinforced everything my dad had taught me.

Rod's favorite word was "Tiger." I never knew Tiger had so many uses. If you did something Rod didn't like, he'd look at you and say, "T-i-i-i-g-r-r" with a mixture of disdain and exasperation in his voice. If you did something he did like, he'd say, "TIGER!!!" his voice ringing with a mixture of excitement and elation.

Rod often used Tiger simply because he couldn't remember the name of the person he was talking to. He was notorious for going to a meeting or a dinner engagement with a few guys, not being able to remember their names, and so introducing them by saying, "Tiger, I want you to meet another Tiger."

The team I played on in 1958 was very talented. More than 20 of us were on full scholarship, 13 went on to sign professional contracts, and six of us made it to the majors.

We were one of the eight teams to qualify for the 1958 College World Series, played at Johnny Rosenblatt Stadium in Omaha, Nebraska.

Having coming into the event with a 23-2 record, we were confident we could win the championship, so we were very surprised and disheartened when we lost in the opening round to Holy Cross. Not only were we shut out, 3-0, but it was the first defeat of the season for our starter, right-hander Bill Thom, who had come into the game with a 7-0 record.

But our optimism returned as we began to pile up victories in the double-elimination tournament — 4-0 over Arizona, 12-1 over Colorado St. College, and 6-2 over Holy Cross in the rematch.

Next up was Missouri, who had won all four of its games. Thom was again on the mound for us and this time, he pitched a three-hit shutout and knocked in three runs himself, with a double in a 7-0 victory. We scored all seven runs in the ninth inning. The win kept us alive, setting up a rematch for the championship.

"We're not going to save a thing," said Missouri coach John "Hi"

Simmons before the game, "not even a dime."

It looked like Simmons would have money left over when his team jumped out to an early 4-0 lead.

Rod knew he had to do something to shake us up, but, with the tension thick in our dugout, yelling at us would only exacerbate the problem. So, as he often did, he chose humor.

With his booming voice, Rod cut through the silence around him by saying, "I wonder what the Bruins are doing tonight."

We may have been in a hole, but, unlike our archrivals who were back home in L.A., we, at least, were there at the World Series with an opportunity to win still in front of us.

We all cracked up, laughter reverberating through the dugout. Relaxed for the moment, we refocused.

And we rallied, scoring seven runs in the fourth, but Missouri caught us by getting three in the eighth to make it 7-7. With two out in that inning, Rod called on his ace, Thom, who had gone the distance the night before. He pitched the rest of the way, going $4^1/3$ innings and allowing only one hit.

Asking a pitcher to go that long after pitching a complete game the day before wouldn't happen today, with pitch-count limitations, but it was a different era then.

Rex Johnston got aboard for us on an infield single to lead off the 12th, went to second on a sacrifice, to third on an infield out, and scored on a single to right by third baseman Mike Blewett to give us an 8-7 victory.

Blewett still has the bat that he used for the winning hit, with the ink from the insignia on the ball still clearly visible on the sweet spot.

It was an historic win, the first College World Series to be decided in extra innings.

Thom was named Most Outstanding Player, deservedly so. Over the final two games, he pitched $13\frac{1}{3}$ consecutive scoreless innings and two victories.

It was truly an honor for me to play for Rod, whose victory in that College World Series was the first of 10 he would win in his 45 seasons as the head coach at USC, including a five-peat, five in a row from 1970 to 1974. No other coach has won more than two straight. In all, Rod took the Trojans to the College World Series 17 times.

In 1999, for qualifying so many times to bring his team to Omaha, site of the College World Series, Rod was presented the key to the city.

Hired by USC in 1942, he would also win 28 conference championships and 1,332 games.

More than 200 of Rod's players went into pro ball, 59 of them making it to the majors. I am on a list of former Trojans that includes the esteemed Tom Seaver, Mark McGwire, Randy Johnson, Fred Lynn, Dave Kingman, Roy Smalley, Don Buford, Rich Dauer, Steve Busby, Jim Barr, and Steve Kemp.

Rod was named coach of the year six times by the American Baseball Coaches Association, and was inducted into ABCA's Hall of Fame in 1970. As part of the commemoration of the 50th anniversary of the College World Series in 1996, he was named head coach of the all-time College World Series team. In 1999, he was named Coach of the Century by Collegiate Baseball and Baseball America.

Commenting on the honor, Rod's good friend, former Dodgers

Manager Tommy Lasorda, joked, "If Rod is really that good, I want to see him win that award back to back."

Rod had a unique style for a baseball coach or manager. He always preferred a light touch whenever possible in dealing with his players. That remark in the dugout in our game against Missouri was typical. In all the years I was around him — 50 in all — I never heard him use a cuss word.

Rod died from complications following a stroke in 2006 at the age of 91.

"I got angry only when somebody introduced Rod as the greatest college baseball coach in the last 100 years," long-time Manager Sparky Anderson told the L.A. Times after Rod's death. "Don't [just] say he's the best college coach. He's one of the greatest baseball coaches in the history of our game."

As for me, I was pleased with my performance in my one year of varsity baseball at USC. I hit .348 and led the team in home runs (9) and RBIs (67). And I was honored with a spot on the College World Series All-Tournament Team and eventually inducted into the USC Athletic Hall of Fame.

So I had been successful at both the high school and collegiate levels.

What next?

It was time to see if I could succeed at the highest level of all.

# Riding the Backroads
# of Baseball

F OR THE FIRST 19 YEARS OF MY LIFE, I did not set foot in a major league stadium because I grew up in Southern California, and the closest major league city was St. Louis, 1,800 miles away.

When I finally did walk into a big league ballpark, it was the Los Angeles Memorial Coliseum, a place where big leaguers had not yet played and many people were not yet ready to accept it as a baseball stadium.

The Coliseum was home to the NFL Rams, and the USC and UCLA football teams, and it was going to be the Dodgers' temporary home while their permanent stadium was being built north of downtown in Chavez Ravine.

I first stepped onto the Coliseum grass in the spring of 1958. With the Dodgers still in spring training in Vero Beach, Florida, the USC baseball team was given the honor of breaking in the makeshift field.

Our coach, Rod Dedeaux, made the arrangements. We were thrilled to be the first team to try out the … shall we say, *unique* if not downright weird, dimensions. It was 250 feet to the barrier in left field, 320 to left center, 425 to straightaway center, 440 to right center, 390 to straightway right, and, down the right-field line, 301 feet.

We took batting practice and hit several balls over the 40-foot screen in left. I don't remember anyone hitting the ball over the right-field fence.

I knew Duke Snider and the other left-handed Dodger hitters were not going to like the setup, but the right-handed batters would love it.

There was nothing the Dodgers could do about it if they were going to play their games in an oval football stadium. But it was the best option at the time until Dodger Stadium was built, and, when 78,672 fans showed up on April 18, 1958, for the first Dodger game in Los Angeles, club officials felt assured they had made the right choice.

I was lucky enough to be part of that crowd and, nearly 60 years later, I can still remember it clearly. It was a special day in L.A. because major league baseball had come to town, and it wasn't just any major league team. It was the Dodgers, the most dominant and colorful team in the National League over the previous decade.

I got to the ballpark early because I wanted to watch the teams take batting practice. The Dodgers looked great in their blue and white uniforms. The sun was shining, the temperature was in the low 70s, and the smell of hot dogs and popcorn was in the air.

The Dodgers beat the San Francisco Giants, 6-5. Carl Erskine was the winning pitcher, and Clem Labine picked up the save. Hooray for Hollywood.

Even though I was on a USC baseball team that would go on to win the College World Series two months later, and even though I hoped to continue my career at the professional level, the thought that, before that season was over, I would be back in the Coliseum wearing a Dodger uniform seemed like a fantasy.

So too, as it turned out, was the thought that the Dodgers would have instant success in their new home and remain among the National League's top teams.

The euphoria instantly faded following Opening Day. They lost the final two games of that series against the Giants, finished April 5-9, were 11-17 in May, and continued on that downward path. The Dodgers finished 71-83, seventh in the then eight-team National League, 21 games behind the league-leading Milwaukee Braves.

I was focused on my own future after the College World Series ended in June. It was seven years before the creation of the major league baseball draft. Back then, teams met with and made offers to anyone they were interested in. I met with a scout from the Chicago White Sox who offered me a contract for $100,000.

My dad asked the scout if someone from the White Sox front office could verify the offer. No one did.

Jerry Gardner, who played minor league baseball with my dad, scouted for the Pittsburgh Pirates. Jerry came to our house in Long Beach one night and told me, "Look, I've got to do this. The Pirates told me to offer you $40,000 to sign, but I wouldn't do it if I was you because you're going to get more than that."

He didn't know that the White Sox had already made their offer.

I politely said thanks, but no thanks.

Jerry smiled, turned to my mom, whom he had known for years, and said, "Marge, how 'bout a cold beer?"

For years afterward, every time I had a big game, Jerry would send a note to the Pirates' scouting department to let them know in great detail what I had done.

When the Dodgers heard about the interest in me, Lefty Phillips, who was scouting for them, asked if he could come to the house and talk to me.

Sure, why not?

As my dad told me before the meeting, "Ron, if you're good enough to play in the major leagues, maybe you could play for the Dodgers here at home. Plus, Duke Snider and Carl Furillo are near the end of their careers, and the Dodgers don't have a steady left fielder."

The offer, extended by Phillips, who would go on to manage the Angels, was for $75,000. It was a three-year $25,000 contract with a $50,000 bonus spread over five years.

Though the money was less than the White Sox had offered, the chance to stay in L.A. and play for my hometown team at the start of an exciting new era was the deciding factor. I knew that if I played well, I would do just fine financially.

I signed a Dodgers contract before June ended.

They sent me to play Class A ball in the Western League for the Des Moines Bruins. Back then, there were far more minor leagues than there are today and thus much stiffer competition in the climb to higher levels. For example, the Dodger organization had 12 minor league affiliates in 1958, ranging from Triple-A down to Class D.

My manager at Des Moines was Roy Hartsfield, who also managed me when I was traded to the Toronto Blue Jays in 1977. In addition to managing the Bruins, Hartsfield, an infielder, also played in 102 games for them that season.

That was a lot to ask of a 25-year-old, but he seemed very mature to me. Of course, I was looking at him through the eyes of a 19-year-old.

I joined the Bruins on the road for their game against the Topeka Hawks. I dropped my bag off at the team hotel and went to the Hawks' home field, Community Baseball Park. I asked a maintenance guy where the visiting clubhouse was. He pointed to a structure but, hell, it wasn't a clubhouse; it was a shack with no lockers, four showerheads including one that didn't work, nails sticking out of the studs in the walls, and three hangers for my clothes.

Welcome to the low minors.

I admit I was spoiled. We had much better facilities at USC.

Hartsfield asked me if I was ready to play, wished me luck, and went over the signs. He warned me that, if reporters asked me why I had bunted or tried to steal, to tell them to talk to him.

"I'm the manager on this team," Hartsfield said. "I'm the one with the fuzzy nuts and I make all the baseball decisions around here."

In other words, play hard and shut up.

My dad told me that when he played, the guys would sit around in the clubhouse after a game and talk about it. Because we had beaten Topeka that day, I figured everybody would be in a good mood and I could get to know my new teammates.

So, I sat there for a few minutes until I suddenly realized everyone else had already showered and dressed. Then I heard the trainer say, "Bus leaves in 20 minutes."

Leaving??? To go where? To the next town, that's where. This dumb rookie didn't know that we had just played the final game of the series.

I took a cold shower because there was no more hot water, packed my bag, and ran out to the bus. I told Hartsfield I had left my luggage at the hotel. "That's OK," he said. "We have to drive by there on the way out of town. You can run in and get your stuff."

The next town was Sioux City, Iowa, and their clubhouse was a little better.

Things began to slow down for me in the days that followed, both on and off the field. I got acquainted with my teammates, was in the lineup every day, was hitting around .300, and playing well defensively.

But life on the road could still be brutal. One trip ended on a Wednesday night in Albuquerque. Thursday was a day off for travel. Our next scheduled game was on Friday in Des Moines. I'll never forget that bus ride. It took us nearly 28 hours to drive from Albuquerque to Des Moines. The bus' peak speed was 60 mph, and that was on a level or downhill road. If there was a little uphill climb, it slowed down as if it were in neutral. I could have run faster carrying my luggage. It was hot, temperatures in the mid 90s, and, even worse, the bus' air-conditioning unit wasn't working.

Adding to the misery, most of my teammates were hungry and had no money to buy food or drinks. Our per diem was just $2. That cash was long gone, and each player's next paycheck was sitting in Des Moines.

It was the road trip from hell. What had I gotten myself into?

We made a pit stop at a small town somewhere in Oklahoma. I had converted a tiny amount of my bonus money into traveler's checks. I cashed one for $100, went into a market, and loaded up on Cokes, beer, ice, bread, bologna, cheese, potato chips, lettuce, mustard, mayonnaise, and a few other edibles.

When we got back on the bus, I sat down across the aisle from our manager and began making sandwiches. The trainer gave me a wooden tongue depressor to use as a knife. I worked as fast as I could, taking a slice of bread and adding bologna, cheese, mustard or mayonnaise, lettuce, and another slice of bread, then passed the sandwiches back down the aisle.

After I had made a dozen or so, Hartsfield leaned over and quietly said, "Redhead, you wouldn't happen to have one of those sandwiches for the skipper, would you?"

I smiled. The skipper was also out of money.

After the guys had their fill, I asked Hartsfield if he would like another sandwich. "No thanks," he said, "but that was a damn fine meal."

We finally arrived at the ballpark in Des Moines the next morning, and the paychecks were waiting for the guys. Some of them didn't even go back to the team hotel. They just slept in the clubhouse and waited for game time.

When the game was over, I checked into the hotel with six or seven other guys on the team. The rooms cost $4 a night, but had no air-conditioning.

I was given a corner room on the second floor. I opened both windows to allow what breeze there was to pass through. It was a lot better than sitting on that bus.

After night games, my entertainment consisted of looking at a bar across the street at closing time. Every night, the owner threw everyone out at 2 a.m.

It seemed like there was always someone who refused to budge. "If you don't get out of here, " the owner told a defiant customer one night, "I'm going to hit you in the mouth.

"You don't have enough guts to hit me," the customer yelled.

Wrong. The owner hit him square in the mouth and down he went.

"You don't have enough guts to do that again," said the customer after staggering to his feet.

Wrong again. The owner popped him again and knocked him back onto the floor.

This time, after slowly pulling himself up, the customer, slurring his words, said, "Now you've pissed me off and I'm not ever coming back to this joint again."

He was there the next night.

Well, the summer heat and humidity finally got to me. I moved into a different hotel, one with air-conditioning, for $9 a day. It was worth the extra five bucks, but I kind of missed the 2 a.m. entertainment across the street.

After 51 games with Des Moines, where I hit .297 with 13 home runs and 41 RBIs, the Dodgers sent me to the St. Paul Saints, one of their AAA teams. Johnny Glenn, the Saints' center fielder, had injured his knee, so I was brought up to take his place on the roster.

I joined the team, a member of the American Association, in Charlotte, North Carolina, and the first thing I noticed was that the clubhouse was much larger and nicer than those in the Western League. The lockers were wider, there were more showerheads, better bathroom facilities, and a full trainer's room.

I was there only for the Saints' last 18 games of the season. Then I was told that I was being called up to the ultimate level, the majors, by the Dodgers.

My clubhouse was about to get even larger.

# 5

## Carl Furillo
## Defends His Turf

I T WAS SEPTEMBER, a time when major league teams can expand their roster to 40 players. I would become one of the 40, as would pitcher Roger Craig, who was also being called up from St. Paul.

Our flight arrived in Philadelphia, where the Dodgers were scheduled to play, around noon on Sept. 9, 1958. There was a big storm passing through the area, and it caused one helluva rough landing for our plane. It was still better than a 28-hour bus ride.

We got our bags, jumped in a taxi, and headed to The Warwick Hotel. As we drove through town, I thought, "I've only played 69 minor league games and now, I'm in the big leagues. I'm going to play for the team I watched on Opening Day at the Coliseum."

When I got to the hotel, I called my dad to tell him I was in Philly with the Dodgers. "Nice going," he said. "Hustle. Try hard. Do the best you can."

He knew I would.

Roger and I went to Connie Mack Stadium, home of the Phillies, early that afternoon. The Dodgers and Phillies had a game suspended earlier in the season, so we first had to finish that one before we could start the regularly scheduled game.

The clubhouse man told me that the manager, Walter Alston, wanted to see me. When I found him, I was greeted by this big, soft-speaking man. He welcomed me to the Dodgers and said he was looking forward to watching me play. Wow — until that moment, I didn't even know if I was actually going to be in a major league game.

Rookie Ron Fairly warms up in the outfield of Connie Mack Stadium in 1958 as Duke Snider, left, and Wally Moon assess his form.

When I asked Mr. Alston what position he wanted me in during batting practice, he said, "Why don't you go to right field tonight."

By the time I put on my uniform and went on the field, the gates had opened and the stands were almost filled. It seemed there were more people rooting for the Dodgers than for the Phillies. I think most of those pulling for us had driven down from Brooklyn.

Those of us who were not in the starting lineup hit first in the batting cage. With five minutes allotted for us, each player got five swings, and, if there was time left, one swing apiece. There was a pecking order. Players who were already on the team hit first, and then guys like me.

I was nervous as hell. I just hoped I wouldn't embarrass myself. Maybe I could even hit a ball hard somewhere. Anywhere.

I reminded myself that I had been swinging a bat since I was barely able to lift one, took a deep breath, timed the pitcher's release, and smacked a few line drives.

Hey, I thought, I can do this. I belong here.

When the next group came in to hit, I trotted out to right field.

Standing there was Carl Furillo, a great fielder with one of the best throwing arms in baseball.

I stood there, not far from Furillo, just happy to shag flies with someone of his stature. He didn't say much at first. After I caught a couple of fly balls, I introduced myself.

"They tell me you're pretty good," he said.

"I don't know about that," I replied. "I'm just excited to be here."

Looking me in the eye, Furillo said, "I want you to know one thing. I'm the right fielder on this team. You can have it when I'm finished with it, but I'm not finished with it yet."

Then he walked away. I didn't expect that kind of reception.

A few minutes later, Duke Snider came over from center field, introduced himself, and welcomed me to the team. He was very friendly, wanting to know what position I played and where I grew up. When I told him I was from Long Beach and went to USC, Duke smiled and told me that he went to Compton High School (his nickname was the Compton Comet), and was a Trojan fan. The conversation was just what I had needed to relax and start to feel part of the team.

Soon, it was time to start the suspended game. The umpires came out, the lineups were announced, the pitchers completed their warmups, and the scoreboard was set at the point play had been suspended. It was a tie score, Phillies batting in the bottom of the ninth inning with two outs and the bases loaded.

Larry Sherry was on the mound for us and Wally Post was the batter.

First pitch landed in the dirt.

Second pitch landed on the roof of the stadium.

Two pitches, one grand slam. My childhood dream of being in uniform in a major league game had come true, but it had lasted only about 30 seconds.

What happened next, though, made up for my disappointment. We all went quietly back into the clubhouse to await the regularly scheduled game. Alston announced the starting lineup and I heard my name. I was batting seventh and playing right field. I was going to play in a full major league game.

Wow.

It shouldn't have been a surprise. I knew it was going to happen. The Dodgers had called me up to see if I could play at this level. But still, seeing my name on the manager's lineup card was surreal.

Maybe that's why Furillo was so rough on me when I met him. Maybe he was trying to toughen me up for what lay ahead.

Before the game started, Duke asked me to play catch with him to get his arm loose. This is amazing, I thought. I'm playing catch with Duke Snider.

Pee Wee Reese and Gil Hodges came up, wished me luck and told me they hoped I'd get a few hits.

All the support was truly appreciated.

In my first major league at-bat, I grounded to first to end an inning. I wound up 0 for 3 in my first major league game. Sandy Koufax was the losing pitcher that night, but he wasn't the Koufax that he was going to become.

Later that evening, I lay in bed recapping what an incredible day I'd had even though I didn't get a hit. I'm in the big leagues, wearing a Dodger uniform, number 55, with teammates whose names I knew from newspapers, television, and radio. Along with those I've already mentioned, the roster included Don Drysdale, Don Newcombe, Carl Erskine, Clem Labine, Don Zimmer, Ed Roebuck, and Jim Gilliam.

I thought of my dad, who played 11 years in the minors, but never got into a big league game.

The next morning around 11 a.m., there was a loud pounding on my door, so forceful that I thought it was going to come off its hinges.

I opened it, and was staring into a belt buckle. It was being worn by Frank Howard, all 6 feet 7 inches and 255 pounds of him.

"Hi, Mr. Fairly," he said, "I'm Frank Howard and I'm your new roommate. Can I come in?"

What was I going to say? No, find another room? There was no way to stop him from coming through the door, even if I had wanted to. He could come through the wall if he wanted to.

"Welcome, Frank," I told him. "Put your stuff on that bed and make yourself at home."

He was so polite that it took two or three days before he felt comfortable calling me Ron instead of Mr. Fairly.

When we got to the ballpark that afternoon, Frank and I discovered that both our names were in the lineup posted on the dugout wall. Frank was in left and I was in center, with Furillo in right.

The starting pitchers were future Hall of Famers, Drysdale and Robin Roberts. We lost, but our room had a good night. I had three hits and Frank had two. How about that? We each got our first major league hit off a Hall of Famer.

A few days later, we were playing the Pirates in Pittsburgh's Forbes Field.

The great Rogers Hornsby was at the ballpark, standing around the batting cage. I do not toss the word "great" around lightly, but this is a player who is considered by many to be the best right-handed hitter to ever play the game. In a career that stretched from 1915 to 1937, mostly with the St. Louis Cardinals, Hornsby, nicknamed "The Rajah," led the National League in batting seven times, including five seasons in a row, hit over .400 three times, and finished up with a career batting average of .358, best ever in the National League, and second only to Ty Cobb (.366) in major-league history.

Standing at the batting cage, I overheard Hornsby ask one of the players what he had done before coming to the stadium that day. Went to the movies, was the answer.

"You shouldn't do that," Hornsby said. "Going to the movies is bad for your eyes."

Replied the player to the 62-year-old Hall of Famer, "But Rajah, the movies don't flicker anymore."

That day with right-hander Ronnie Kline on the mound for the Pirates, I hit my first major league home run. It was only about 300 feet down the right-field line at Forbes Field, but closer to 375 to right center. The ball I hit traveled only around 310 feet before landing in the seats. Later in the game, Duke hit a high drive that sailed easily over the 375-foot sign, landing in the upper deck. That ball had to have traveled around 440 feet.

The next day, a story in the local newspaper read, "Ron Fairly and Duke Snider hit home runs in the same place."

In my month with the Dodgers, I learned a lot from the established players about opposing pitchers. How hard did they throw? What did the trajectory of their breaking ball look like? What would each pitcher most likely throw in a jam? I got answers to those questions and more, sometimes even before I had a chance to ask.

And then, it was over, less than a month after I had arrived. I felt like the season ended way too quickly for me. For most of the Dodgers, however, it couldn't end quickly enough, considering the team finished in seventh place.

As excited as I had been to reach the majors, I had one more unforgettable moment after I returned home.

At the L.A. airport to pick someone up, I spotted Ted Williams standing at a newsstand.

"Mr. Williams, excuse me," I said, "my name is Ron Fairly and I just signed with the Dodgers this past summer."

That's as far as I got because Ted interrupted me to say, "I know who you are. You're a left-handed hitter out of USC."

My mouth dropped open. I didn't know what to say. Everyone knew who Ted Williams was, but how in the world did he know who I was?

"Because," he told me, "I always follow young hitters coming out of the Southern California area."

We visited for a couple of minutes, then he excused himself, wished me luck, and left to board his flight.

How about that — Ted Williams had heard of *me*.

# 6

## Hanging With Duke, Pee Wee, and Gil in Zero Beach

A MONTH BEFORE spring training started, I received a phone call from Carl Furillo. Remember, he was the player who told me, on the day I reported to the Dodgers, that he wasn't ready just yet to relinquish his position.

Now, he was asking me if I would like to come to Dodgertown, the team's spring training headquarters in Vero Beach, Florida, a couple of weeks early to work out in the mornings and do some fishing in the afternoons. I didn't have any fishing equipment or experience, but I said, yes, sure. Sounded like a great opportunity to get an early jump on the others who were hoping to make the team.

Most of the players called up at the end of the season are sent back down to the minor leagues the next spring, and that included me.

I still had to prove to the front office, the manager, and the coaches that I could play at the major league level. Part of that was showing them how much I wanted to play.

When I landed in Melbourne, someone from Dodgertown picked me up and drove me to Vero Beach, 34 miles south. Entering the Dodgers' facility, I saw old, gray barracks along the road surrounded by row upon row of orange and grapefruit trees. Frankly, I was expecting something a little nicer.

In 1929, a local businessman named Bud Holman was one of the key movers and shakers in the decision to build an airport in Vero Beach. When World War II broke out, the U.S. Navy, looking for a place on the Florida coast to set up a flight training base, chose Vero Beach, partly because it had the airfield. The Navy commissioned the Vero Beach Naval Air Station in 1942 and built those barracks to house 2,700 Navy and Marine personnel, and 300 WAVES and female Marines. The airport was enlarged from 100 to 2,500 acres.

The sky was soon filled with dive-bomber and fighter pilots training for duty overseas, but unfortunately, more than 100 of them lost their lives in flight-training exercises originating from that site. Though they never left our shores, their sacrifice was every bit as meaningful as those of the hundreds of thousands of Americans who lost their lives in combat overseas.

When the war ended, the facility was turned back to the city. The timing was just right because the Dodgers were looking for a training facility. Holman, convinced they would be the ideal tenant for the property, contacted Branch Rickey, then president of the team, who sent Buzzie Bavasi, then the general manager of the Dodgers' minor league team in Nashua, New Hampshire, down to look at Vero Beach and several other Florida sites. Holman wasn't about to let this big fish get away from his coastal city. He lobbied hard, making the case that there was enough land to handle the more than 600 ballplayers in the organization, and the necessary housing, in the form of the Navy barracks, was already built.

Holman also included a name for the site in his proposal: Dodgertown.

Bavasi bought in to the idea, and so did Mr. Rickey. "We had our own plane then and we could walk from the airport to [Dodgertown]," said Bavasi. "The other places were trying to sell us something. Vero Beach was trying to give us something."

A key factor for Mr. Rickey was the fact that Jackie Robinson, who broke the color barrier when he joined the team in 1947, would be free in Dodgertown of the segregation he would be subjected to in other southern sites in Florida.

In 1948, the Dodgers held their first spring training in Dodgertown.

When Walter O'Malley, who became team president in 1950, decided to build a small stadium in Dodgertown in 1953, he returned the favor to the man who had named the facility, naming the ballpark Holman Stadium.

46

Wandering around the facility in my first trip there in 1959, I found the team offices, a lobby, and a cafeteria situated in the middle of the barracks. In the lobby were two pool tables, several lounging chairs, and card tables surrounded by large photos of Dodger greats past and present on the walls.

Our rooms in the barracks had no heating or air-conditioning. The major league players stayed in what had been the officers' quarters while the minor league players were in the rooms that had housed noncommissioned servicemen. In the major league section, two players were assigned to each unit, which had separate bedrooms. The showers, plastered with stucco, were so small that you had to stand diagonally if you didn't want to scrape your elbows on the walls.

The floors were wooden. At night, you could hear the steps of anyone walking down the halls.

Carl, having arrived the day before, left me a message at the front desk to meet him in the clubhouse at 9 a.m. to work out. I couldn't wait. I was there at 8.

The exterior walls of the clubhouse were painted gray with Dodger blue trim. Inside, the rectangular room, like the rooms in the barracks, was small with no insulation in the walls. There were small, wood-framed lockers along the walls with chicken wire separating them. There was just enough room to hang your street clothes and one uniform. When I got there, uniforms were hanging in the lockers even though they wouldn't be needed for several more weeks. A strip of tape with a player's name on it was attached to the top of each locker and, alongside, a dozen of his personal bats. Large trunks filled with baseball equipment and a potbellied stove sat in the middle of the room. I got a rush of adrenaline just seeing all those blue and white uniforms.

Yes, the clubhouse was small and old, and reeked with the smell of baseball, but I loved it.

I went into the trainer's room, which was also small, containing only two rubbing tables and a whirlpool. There, I met Doc Wendler, one of the trainers.

In walked our clubhouse man, John "The Senator" Griffin. He tipped the scales at close to 300 pounds, had a four-day beard, and a cigar hanging out of his mouth.

"What are you doing here?" he asked. "Spring training doesn't start for another two weeks."

"I'm here to work out and go fishing with Carl Furillo," I said.

"OK, but throw your wet towels in the towel bin," Griffin replied, "and don't make a mess."

And with that, he walked out.

When Carl showed up, we went out to one of the fields, did some hitting against the Iron Mike pitching machine, went through fielding drills, then headed to the nearby Indian River for an afternoon of fishing. Carl loved to fish and he taught me to love it as well, showing me everything from how to make my own lures to the best poles to use and how to bait my hook. We would bring what we caught, mostly bluefish and tarpon, back to Dodgertown, where the team cooks prepared the fish for our dinner and took what was left home to their own families.

Sometimes, we would go fishing with Jerry Hatfield, a buddy of Carl who was born in Vero Beach, owned a fruit packing company, and knew every sandbar and fishing hole on the Indian River. He had a house on one of the canals around Vero Beach, and kept his boat anchored a few feet away.

I don't know what I enjoyed more, practicing on the diamond or fishing with Carl and Jerry. It was the most relaxing way possible to get ready for the arduous season ahead. Playing for the Dodgers sure had its benefits.

Those peaceful, lazy days on the river showed me that Carl, although he was one of the strongest, toughest men I ever met, had a soft side to him as well.

He was at the end of his career and would be out of baseball in two years while I was just beginning. But the gap in years didn't affect our relationship. We became good friends, bonded by, I believe, mutual respect.

Carl could be an SOB, but the rough edges of his personality fueled his passion and devotion to the game. He taught me a lot about playing the outfield and hitting. In those first few days I was in Vero, he worked with me tirelessly on getting to a ball quickly and making the kind of throw that could either cut down a runner or least prevent him from getting an extra base. He knew what he was talking about. He played his position flawlessly and had one of the most powerful arms of any

48

outfielder in baseball. Born in a suburb of Reading, Pennsylvania, he earned the nickname "The Reading Rifle" for his bullet throws from right field.

After I got to know him, I understood why he staked out his territory the first time I met him. In his best-selling book, "The Boys of Summer," Roger Kahn wrote of Furillo, "Right field in Brooklyn was his destiny."

Carl wore the number six on his jersey and, when he left the Dodgers, I asked if I could wear that number out of respect for him. I wore it proudly for years and, in addition to paying tribute to him, it motivated me. I felt that if I was going to wear his number, I had to play like him.

When I was traded from the Dodgers to the Montreal Expos, I told Nobe Kawano, our clubhouse manager, "If you give this number to someone, make sure it's someone who can hit." He gave it to Steve Garvey, who was definitely a solid hitter. To this day, whenever

When Carl Furillo left the Dodgers, Ron, shown here at Dodgertown at Vero Beach, requested his No. 6 jersey. The sleeves are two inches shorter than the standard jersey because Furillo liked his arms free, and Ron followed the leader. Over 57 years, only Furillo, Fairly, and Steve Garvey wore that number for the Dodgers.

I see Steve, I say, "Hi, Six" or "Hi, Half Dozen." For 57 years, only Carl, Steve, and I wore that number. It bothers me when it's given to a Dodger who is not a good hitter. I'll bet if you ask Steve, he will say the same thing.

The tranquil hours on the Indian River were cut back drastically when spring training officially started. Along with Carl and me, there were suddenly more than 600 other players taking the field, counting the minor leaguers. Branch Rickey had created the farm system during his days with the Cardinals, and he placed just as much emphasis on it when he joined the Dodgers in late 1942. It was still flourishing and creating bumper crops of young prospects long after Rickey and the Dodgers were gone from Brooklyn.

We had 9½ diamonds, sliding pits, batting cages, and a dozen pitching mounds. The schedules were tight. Every half-hour, teams would rotate from location to location. Each day was different, with one group going to the batting cages, another to live batting, a third to infield practice. The pitchers threw off one of the many mounds, or ran.

I said there were characters in baseball, and Herman Levy was certainly one of them. Herman worked for the post office in Brooklyn and also, during the summer, at Ebbets Field, when it was still standing. Every spring, he took time off to drive to Dodgertown. It was a paid vacation for him. He got out of New York's cold weather, got a roof over his head, and a paycheck from the Dodgers.

Herman had several duties, but, befitting his day job, was primarily in charge of the mail. When players would see Herman, they would ask if they had any mail. He always answered by telling them exactly how many letters they had received. It was amazing that he could remember the names of more than 600 players and staff, and how much mail each had received that particular day.

In addition, he kept track of everybody's laundry when it came back from the cleaners.

Outside the Dodger offices was a flagpole and, every morning at 7, you could hear him, from a hundred feet away, reciting the Pledge of Allegiance.

At Ebbets Field, Herman worked as an usher or took tickets at one of the gates.

One day, they put him in charge of parking cars in a small lot that held 60 vehicles just across the street from the ballpark. Herman was told to collect $2 for each car. He parked the cars himself. When the lot was full, he allowed more cars to come in, an extra 20 in all. So instead of the usual total of $120, he had collected $160.

But there was a price to pay for that profit. The cars were parked so close together that it wasn't possible to open the doors of some of them. It was particularly annoying to fans who had left the game early, but had to stand around and wait for the final out, when the cars around them would begin to move.

As bad as that was, it was even worse for customers who found dents and scrapes on their cars, costing the Dodgers thousands of dollars in repair costs.

That was the last day Herman parked cars.

Another of my favorite characters was Art Fowler, a pitcher for the Dodgers and Angels. He was from South Carolina, and had a deep southern drawl and a wonderful sense of humor.

Art hated running drills, and in spring training, Joe Becker, the Dodgers pitching coach, ran the pitchers in the outfield until their tongues hung out. Joe claimed that "running makes your legs strong, and strong legs help win games."

One hot day, Art had had enough running, and hollered at Becker, "Joe, if running is so important to winning, how come Jesse Owens didn't win 20 games?"

Art liked to spin stories about his native state. "I got a fishing hole back home that's so good," he'd say, "you have to bait your hook behind a tree."

One day, Art was mowing his front yard. He got thirsty, and decided to have a beer. He rode his lawn mower off the yard and down the street to a local tavern, where he refreshed himself with three or four beers. He did quench his thirst, but at some cost — riding the mower back home, a police officer stopped him and cited him for driving under the influence on a public street.

We were taking batting practice one afternoon on the main field, when Duke Snider asked if I would like to play golf after practice. Of course I said yes.

"We're playing with Pee Wee and Gil," said Duke.

Workouts started at 10 a.m. and we were generally finished by 3. For the balance of the morning, all I could think about was that I was going to play golf with Duke Snider, Gil Hodges, and Pee Wee Reese, who had become a coach by then. These were people I had only known from reading the newspaper or watching TV.

We went to the Vero Beach Country Club and, although I was nervous, I hit my first tee shot as far as I could hit a golf ball. I admired it as if it were a towering home run to center field.

As we walked down the fairway, Gil kept telling me how good my tee shot was, and asked if that was the longest drive I had ever hit.

When we got to my ball, Gil said, "That was a great tee shot, Ron. ... You're away," meaning that I was farthest from the hole among the four of us. I looked at Gil's ball and saw that he had hit his shot 20 yards farther than mine. I looked back at him and saw a big grin on his face. He had stuck the needle in me pretty good.

After we played the 18 holes, the four of us visited the 19th hole for a cold beer. We sat there talking about our golf game, then Pee Wee switched the conversation to baseball. He started talking about his theories on hitting, about the necessity for a player to accept his strengths and limitations. Duke and Gil jumped in on the conversation and offered their input.

When they all finished, Pee Wee turned to me and said, "Ron, what is your approach to hitting with runners in scoring position?" He caught me tongue-tied. I hadn't been thinking about myself because I was so engrossed in listening to these accomplished professionals. Finally, I blurted out that I try to get a pitch to hit hard somewhere.

"Well," said Pee Wee, "we'll get a chance to see what you can do."

No pressure there.

I lay in bed that night thinking about how lucky I was. How many people would pay money to play golf with those guys, and get innovative ideas on how to hit.

Two or three days later, we were playing the Detroit Tigers in an exhibition game and I was coming up late in the game with two outs and the tying run at second.

Before I got to the plate, I heard Pee Wee holler at me, "Hey, remember what we talked about the other day. Show me."

Talk about great expectations. Now, I'm not just some rookie walking up for an ordinary spring training at-bat; I have to do something to impress Dodger legend Pee Wee Reese.

I worked the count in my favor, two balls and one strike. The next pitch was a fastball, and I jumped on it and hit a hard line drive to center. But the center fielder charged in and caught the ball chest high for an easy out.

The Tigers won, but I don't recall much about the game except the vivid memory of walking back to the clubhouse deeply disappointed that I didn't drive in that run.

When I came in, Pee Wee was waiting for me at my locker. "Ron," he said, patting me on the back, "that was a very good at-bat. Keep hitting the ball like that and you'll drive in a lot of runs."

He really lifted my spirits because if Pee Wee said I had a good at-bat, then I had a good at-bat.

Every player remembers their home runs and other big hits, but how many remember their outs? That was one I will never forget because Pee Wee gave me confidence that I could hit the ball hard in a close game, and not all of them would be outs.

Today, Vero Beach is home to nearly 17,000 residents. Its economy depends heavily on the citrus industry and tourism. It is also the administrative and manufacturing headquarters for Piper Aircraft. It has many fine restaurants and, among its numerous hotels, is Disney's Vero Beach Resort.

That's a lot different from the town I saw when I arrived in 1959. There was so little to do there back then that players sometimes referred to it as Zero Beach.

Dodgertown was 4 miles from downtown and pretty isolated. We had no radio or television in the barracks. There were a couple of good restaurants in town at that time, but who had enough money to eat out?

After workouts, it was either golf, fish, or sleep. That was about it.

Most of the players didn't make enough to rent cars, so, in the evenings, there wasn't much to do but sit in the lounge outside the cafeteria and talk baseball, or play pool or cards with 600 other players who had nothing to do.

It didn't matter in the first week or two of spring training because most of the guys were worn out after the daily four- or five-hour regimen that the coaches put us through. They were too tired and stiff to do much more than lie around, or maybe watch TV in the lobby.

Unlike today, when players are already in shape when they report to camp, spring training when I played was about losing weight and firming up muscles to regain the strength and stamina they had the previous season. Back in those days, players didn't make enough money to devote themselves to staying in shape during the offseason. To support their families, they had to get real jobs, like selling insurance or working in construction. Guys couldn't afford to spend all winter in a gym, or hire trainers.

As we began to acclimate ourselves to the workout routine, the soreness started to fade from our bodies and our energy level rose. That's when boredom crept in. Players became tired of just hanging around the barracks. It was time to test the curfew.

To avoid players coming in at all hours of the night, there was a curfew of 11 p.m. for minor league players and midnight for the major leaguers. The punishment for violating curfew was a $100 fine.

The coaches and minor league managers were responsible for enforcing the curfew. The only entrances to the barracks were at each end of the buildings. The coaches and managers would hide behind trees or bushes to catch anyone coming in late.

One dark night, Roy Hartsfield, my old minor league manager at Des Moines, and Rube Walker were on duty. Four or five minor leaguers came strolling in late, trying to be as quiet as possible. Hartsfield spotted them before they reached the barracks door and told them to stop, but they took off running. Hartsfield and Walker chased after them, but the players were too fast.

Walker and Hartsfield quickly ran out of gas. Walker, breathless, called off the chase, telling Hartsfield they weren't going to catch anybody.

"I know that," Hartsfield said. "I don't care about the curfew. I just want to know who that kid out in front is so I can try to get him on my team this year. He could be a great base stealer."

Johnny Podres was one of the players known to stay out late and miss curfew.

One morning, Buzzie Bavasi, our general manager, came storming into the clubhouse and started hollering at Podres, who was sitting in front of his locker sipping coffee and reading the racing form.

"Johnny," said Buzzie, "if you come into your room at two in the morning, play that damn record player of yours, and wake me up again, I'll fine you $500."

Johnny thought quickly, weighed the $100 fine for being out after curfew versus the $500 fine for waking up his general manager and came to a logical decision.

"Buzzie," said Johnny, "that wasn't me last night because I wasn't in yet."

Johnny never changed. In 1991, he became the Phillies' pitching coach under Manager Jim Fregosi. In spring training, Johnny called the pitching staff together and asked which of them liked to drink and chase women. Some of the pitchers raised their hands.

"OK," Johnny said, "you guys will be the starters because I'll only need you once every four or five days. The rest of you will be the relievers."

There was a bar called Lenny's West within walking distance of Dodgertown. We would go there at night to relax and talk baseball. We didn't drink much, but the place had air-conditioning and everyone was friendly.

One night, with curfew approaching, three players got into their car to head back to the barracks, but nothing happened when the driver tried to start it. The battery was dead.

No big deal, they figured. They'd take the short walk back to Dodgertown and pick the car up the next day.

There was a short cut on a dirt road that weaved around one of the far baseball fields and then led to the barracks.

It was dark that night, so dark that it was hard for them to see their own feet. Fortunately, before they stepped on it, they were able to spot something suddenly moving several feet away. They gasped, frozen for an instant. An 8- or 9-foot alligator was staring back at them.

Scared as hell, they took off running and, in just a couple of minutes, were all safely back in their rooms. They had never run that fast in their lives. Not even on the base paths.

After that, every player who drove to Lenny's West made sure he had a flashlight in his car.

A lot of the players loved to bet at the racetrack, as did Buzzie. A couple of the guys were close to some jockeys, enabling them to get inside information now and then.

One spring in early March, Don Zimmer got a hot tip on a horse that would be running in the seventh race at Hialeah Park Race Track. "We can get great odds," Zimmer told everybody, "and it's guaranteed that he'll win."

We were told the horse was strong, had looked great in workouts, and the race was a mile and a quarter, an ideal length for him. There were a lot of good reasons to plop some money down on this horse.

A lot of guys jumped on this opportunity. Money was coming in from everywhere. Everybody on the major league roster placed a bet.

It took several of us pleading our case to get Alston to shorten our day's work so that we could get down to Hialeah, 145 miles south of Vero Beach, in time to place our bets.

On the day of the race, 10 of us drove down in three cars. Players who couldn't make the trip gave us money to bet for them. If our horse won, we figured we would have to hire a Brink's truck to bring back all the cash.

We got there early enough to catch a couple of other races before, what for us, was the main event. I bet a couple of bucks on the third and the fourth races and lost both.

Didn't bother me because I was sure I was going to win it all back later.

Our horse's name was Orion, and the odds as post time approached were 8-1. We placed our bets and positioned ourselves on the rail right near the finish line.

Everything seemed perfect.

When the bugle sounded and the horses came out on the track, a big, beautiful golden palomino came out of the paddock. It looked like Trigger, and I wouldn't have been surprised if Roy Rogers was riding him.

Even better, it was Orion. Our horse.

All the others in the race looked like Shetland ponies in comparison.

The jockeys' feet on those horses were almost dragging on the ground.

Boy, were we feeling good.

That feeling stayed with us when the race began with Orion bursting out of the gate.

The horses raced by the grandstand for the first time, and our big guy was in front. Around the first turn, he led by half a length; on the far turn, his lead was up to a length; on the back side, he was ahead by seven or eight lengths, and at the next turn, he was running away from the pack, his lead having increased to 10 lengths. He was approaching the stretch in front by a full 15 lengths. I was counting my money.

And then, it happened.

All of a sudden, Orion slowed down, made a sharp right turn and bolted back toward the stable. Zimmer, Podres, Drysdale, and I stood on the railing looking back down the track at our horse. While the other horses were crossing the finish line, Orion was running in the opposite direction, then disappeared into the stable.

Jaws dropping, profanities spewing, we couldn't believe what we had just seen. Barring an accident, how many horses leading at the final turn don't even cross the finish line?

Then we knew why Orion was an 8-1 longshot.

My first reaction was to announce I was done betting on the ponies.

We did not want to go back to Vero Beach to face the taunts of our teammates after assuring one and all that we would be galloping to the pay window to collect on a sure thing.

How long did our decision to give up betting last? As long as it took for us to tear up our betting slips and let them blow away in the breeze. After all, if we could at least recoup some of our losses, we would have something to show for our embarrassing trip.

How? The dog track. Maybe our luck with horses had run out, but we decided to stop on the way home at a track where we could wager on the greyhounds. Maybe that's where lady luck had gone.

We got to the track in time for the last race. I spotted a dog on the racing sheet named O'Reilly, a 35-1 longshot, and I put $10 down on him to win.

As the race began, O'Reilly was dead last. At least I wouldn't have my heart broken in the stretch as it had been with Orion.

I had kissed my $10 goodbye, when, in the stretch, the lead dog stumbled and fell, and all of the other dogs behind crashed into him, leaving a pile in the middle of the track.

Actually, not all of the other dogs. Because O'Reilly was so far back, he was able to slow down, see what was happening, leap over the pile, and continue at a leisurely pace until he crossed the finish line.

Podres was pissed because his dog had been in the lead, and wound up on the bottom of that pile. Seeing me cheer on O'Reilly caused Johnny to turn his anger at me.

He was having a bad day. First, he lost when his horse chose the stable over the finish line, and then his dog, also in front, fell down.

In his frustration, Johnny started shouting at me, "What a dumb ass bet," he yelled. "Why would you bet on that dog?"

With a big smile on my face, I said, "Because his name is O'Reilly and it's almost St. Patrick's Day."

It felt a lot better coming back to Vero with the $350 I had just won in my pocket.

But that weird and wild day was not quite over. I was in a car being driven back to Dodgertown by Don Miles, an outfielder who had spent three seasons in the minors, had been called up by the Dodgers the previous September, and was now hoping to stick with the club.

You never knew what Donnie was going to say, but it was always entertaining.

One night in batting practice when he was playing for the Victoria Rosebuds of the Texas League, Donnie told his teammates, "I've got me a new batting stance that's so good, the pitchers may never get me out again."

In the game, he struck out six times.

But, blessed with power and speed, the 6-foot-1-inch 210-pounder had put up good numbers for the Rosebuds that season. In 102 games, he batted .325 with 18 home runs and 77 RBIs.

Before spring training, Donnie had married the daughter of Tom O'Connor, Jr., owner of the Rosebuds. She was worth several million dollars, so money was not a big concern for Donnie, as quickly became obvious.

When he arrived in Vero Beach, he decided he didn't want to stay in the barracks, so he asked a local real estate broker to find him a place to rent for up to $2,500 a month. At that time, you could have rented the entire city of Vero Beach for $10,000 a month.

That night at the dog track, four of us — Donnie, Johnny, pitcher Stan Williams, and I — had lingered long after the others had departed. Not wanting to miss curfew, we were anxious to get back, and Donnie was going a little over the speed limit, but not much. Suddenly, out of nowhere, came this flashing blue light. It was a state trooper.

Donnie pulled off to the side, and when the trooper came to his window, this is how the conversation went.

Trooper: You guys are going pretty fast.

Donnie: I have a big engine and I can go faster if I want to.

Johnny: Donnie, shut up. We were speeding.

Trooper: You know if you go too fast, I can call ahead to other cars.

Donnie: I have a radio in my other car.

Johnny: Donnie, shut up and listen to the officer.

At this point, Johnny, Stan, and I are envisioning a night in a jail cell with Buzzie refusing to bail us out.

Trooper: Where are you guys going and why are you in such a hurry?

Donnie: We're major league baseball players with the Los Angeles Dodgers headed back to Vero Beach, and we want to get there before curfew.

Trooper: Speeding is very dangerous and the fine could get up to $100.

Donnie: I have a lot of $100 bills.

Trooper: I'm sure you do.

Donnie: Are you married?

Trooper: Yes, one son and another on the way.

Donnie: My wife is pregnant, too.

Every time the trooper said something, Donnie tried to top him.

Stan: Donnie, stop it. We're in enough trouble and we've got to get back to Vero.

Relief spread over us when the conversation became friendly as the trooper started telling us about his baseball career in high school and college.

About that time, Stan said he had to urinate and asked if it was OK to go in the bushes.

Trooper jokingly: Yeah, but it will cost you another hundred bucks.

Donnie: OK, everybody out of the car and take a leak.

So that's what we did. As we were getting back in, Donnie pulled out a wad of money he had won at the dog track and handed the trooper five $100 bills.

Trooper: I can't accept this money. That's against the law.

Donnie: I don't care. A deal is a deal, no matter what the law says. I gave you my word and that's it.

The trooper tried to give the money back, but Donnie wouldn't accept it. "We don't have time to argue," he said. "We have to get back to Vero Beach before curfew."

Donnie thanked the trooper, hit the gas, and off we went.

I can still see that trooper standing on the side of the highway trying to figure out why he didn't give us a ticket and how he ended up with five $100 bills in his hand.

We made it back to the barracks with 10 minutes to spare before curfew.

Among my favorite moments in Dodgertown were those I spent in Campy's Bullpen.

A Hall of Fame catcher, three-time National League MVP, and one of the leaders of the Brooklyn Dodgers, Roy Campanella never got to be a Los Angeles Dodger. He had been so excited about the opportunity to help lead his team, the only big league team he had ever played for, into this new phase of its existence.

But that opportunity was lost forever on a cold January night in 1958. Campy was driving home at 3 a.m. from the liquor store he owned in Harlem to his Glen Cove, Long Island, home. He skidded on a wet road a mile from his house. His car crashed into a telephone pole and flipped over.

Campy had two fractured vertebrae. It took five surgeons to perform the 4½ hour operation that saved his life.

Had the injury occurred one inch higher, he would probably not have survived.

As it was, at the age of 36, Campy was paralyzed from the shoulders down. He was scheduled to report to Vero Beach just two weeks later, when, for the first time, he would have put on a blue Dodger cap that, instead of the familiar letter B emblazoned in white on the front, would have had the now familiar interlocked letters L and A.

It would have been understandable if Campy had never returned to Vero Beach after that. I can't imagine how painful it must have been for him to sit in his wheelchair and watch his teammates run and throw and swing a bat knowing that he would never again be able to even stand on a baseball field.

Yet Campy did return, not just as a spectator, but as an active participant, an unofficial coach still contributing, still leading.

Every evening, he would sit outside the kitchen and talk baseball with anyone who dropped by. He told stories about his playing days, teaching so many of us about baseball in particular and life in general.

Campy was particularly good with the younger players like me. During the day, he would watch us work out and, in the evening, he would critique our performance.

He came up to the Dodgers in 1948, a year after Jackie Robinson had broken baseball's color barrier. Knowing the kind of pressure Campy, another black man, had been under to produce, and what he accomplished, we were eager to listen to this legendary figure we held in awe.

"Now lookie here, young man," he would say before giving advice or asking us questions. He told young catchers how to block pitches in the dirt, and how to set up hitters. He made us think about game situations. "The count was two balls and no strikes," he would say about an at-bat one of us had in a game earlier that day. "Why did you swing at that pitch low and outside? Wait for a better pitch. Give yourself a chance. The next pitch might be right down the middle of the plate."

Spring training is a good time to learn about prospects on other teams who may soon be coming up to the big club. The Dodgers, like every other team, were anxious to test these guys when they had a bat in their hands.

One spring when Campy was still playing, a highly touted young player was in the opposing lineup.

The first time the player came up, Campy, crouching behind home plate, said, "I'm told you're a pretty good hitter and we're going to find out. This at-bat, we're going to throw you nothing but fastballs to see how you handle them."

The young player hammered out a base hit.

The next time up, Campy complimented the player. "Nice going," the Dodger catcher said. "Looks like you can handle the fastball. This time, we're throwing you nothing but curveballs. Let's see what you can do."

Whack, another base hit.

Third time up, Campy told the young player, "That's good hitting. You've shown us that you can hit the fastball and the curve. Now, we're going to see how you hit lying down."

Meaning that we're going to knock you on your ass with an inside pitch and see how you hit after that.

"You should have seen the look on his face," Campy told me, "when I said that."

Hard lesson learned, the very essence of spring training.

# 7

## The Pebble
## That Won a Championship

T HE ESTABLISHED PLAYERS look forward to the end of spring training with joy. The meaningless games and tedious workouts are over. It's time to play ball for real.

But for the young players like I was in 1959, the end of spring training is a time of anxiety. Which of us will survive as the big league roster is cut down to 28 players for Opening Day, and then down to 25 after a month?

That April, Duke Snider had fluid in his knee and could be used only sparingly. Carl Furillo had pulled a calf muscle and couldn't run. So I made the opening-day roster. When Duke and Carl were back at full strength, I was to be sent down to the minors to play for one of the organization's three Triple-A teams.

Opening on the road against the Cubs, we arrived in Chicago a day and a half before the season was to start, and checked into the Conrad Hilton Hotel. When they handed out the room assignments, I was thrilled when Duke's name was followed by mine. This was not only a guy I had followed through the media for years, but someone who had been so nice and helpful to me since the day I had joined the team.

I didn't get much sleep that night. A year ago, I had been at the Coliseum as a spectator for the Dodgers' first game in Los Angeles. Now, I was going to be at their 1959 Opening Day, not just to watch, but to be a part of it. When my teammates and I arrived at Wrigley Field, I found out just how big a part. When Alston posted the starting lineup on the dugout wall, there was my name.

At the very top. Not only was I starting, but I was batting leadoff.

It was cold when I came out for batting practice, but it didn't bother me. I was so pumped up, I didn't feel anything but the adrenaline surge.

During batting practice, Duke came up and said, "Ron, the reason you're leading off is because we want you to get the hell out of our way. We don't want you to stop a rally."

Duke laughed as he walked away, but there weren't many more laughs when the game began. We got a total of only six hits, and lost 6-1, with Drysdale, the losing pitcher, driving in our only run with a third-inning homer.

At least I had enjoyed a special moment coming up as the first batter, kicking off the game and the season, but it was a feeling I never experienced again. Oh, I went on to enjoy a long and rewarding career — in all, I played in 2,442 major league games. But that was the only time in my career that I batted leadoff to start a season.

When it was time to trim the roster to the 25-man limit, the Dodgers decided to keep me and send someone else down because I had gotten off to a good start, hitting above .300.

For the first time, I felt like I had really made it.

I never experienced the joy of playing in Brooklyn, and the wild and wacky environment of Ebbets Field, having come up a year after the team left. But I feel so fortunate that I was able to play a few seasons with some of the key figures of the Dodgers' final decade in that borough.

Pee Wee Reese, the team captain when I joined the team, had retired at the end of the 1958 season, but stuck around one more year to serve as third-base coach. That gave me an opportunity to soak up some more of his wisdom and knowledge of the game.

Even while he was still playing, Pee Wee didn't yell and scream when he was upset about the team's performance. He spoke calmly and succinctly, but was very effective at getting his message across.

If he didn't feel players were working as hard as they could because of poor concentration or lack of enthusiasm, he would tell them, "Fellas, you've got to show me you want to play. If you don't, take your uniform off and give it to someone who does."

Pee Wee wouldn't single out a particular player, but would speak in terms of the team as a whole.

He had a saying I just loved: "Rush in and out of the clubhouse, and you'll rush in and out of baseball." In other words, players who show up at the ballpark late and leave early don't last long in this game.

Pee Wee's words and advice might have been new to me, but he had been inspiring young players for more than a decade.

"In 1947," Duke told me, "the Dodgers brought me up from St. Paul. I had only been with the big league club a short time when, caught in a situation where I had two strikes on me, I choked up a couple of inches on the bat to protect the plate. On the next pitch, I popped the ball up into left field for an easy out.

"When I returned to the dugout, Pee Wee said to me, 'Duke, what in the hell are you trying to do up there?'

" 'Pee Wee,' I told him, 'I'm just trying to protect the plate and not strike out.'

" 'No, no, no,' Pee Wee replied, 'I'm someone who has to hit like that, but you're not. Swing from your ass. You're not a singles hitter. You're a home run hitter. Don't get cheated. You have so much power. We don't care if you strike out a few times. Swing the damn bat.' "

It was a talk that affected Duke for the rest of his career.

"After that," he said, "I did what Pee Wee told me to do. I swung hard every time."

And wound up hitting 407 home runs.

The most important move Pee Wee ever made came at first base, but it had nothing to do with beating out an infield grounder or tagging a player in a rundown.

Actually, according to Brooklyn right-hander Rex Barney, it occurred with time out as the Dodgers were taking the field in a game against the Reds in Cincinnati.

It was 1947, the year Branch Rickey brought Jackie Robinson up to the Dodgers as the first black man to play in the major leagues. The stories of the verbal abuse Jackie faced that year, the threats of a strike by some opposing players, the disdain and rejection he received on so many occasions, are well-known. Even some people with the Dodgers objected to his presence on the roster.

But during this lull in the game before the bottom half of the first inning, Pee Wee stepped forward to counteract the hateful behavior with a simple gesture. A southerner from segregated Louisville in the neighboring state of Kentucky, Pee Wee was being lambasted by the crowd for even agreeing to be on the same field as Jackie.

"I was warming up on the mound," said Barney in the book "Bums," by Pete Golenbock, "and I could hear the Cincinnati players screaming at Jackie, 'You sonofabitch, you shoeshine boy' and all the rest… While Jackie was standing by first base, Pee Wee went over to him and put his arm around him as if to say, 'This is my boy. This is the guy. We're gonna win with him.' Well, it drove the Cincinnati players right through the ceiling, and you could have heard the gasp from the crowd as he did it."

Although some historians question if the incident really happened, Jackie himself, in a 1949 story in the Brooklyn Eagle, said, "Pee Wee kind of sensed the hopeless, dead feeling in me and came over and stood beside me for a while. He didn't say a word, but he looked over at the chaps who were yelling at me through him and just stared. He was standing by me, I could tell you that.

"Slowly, the jibes died down like when you kill a snake an inch at a time, and then, there was nothing but quiet from them. It was wonderful the way this little guy did it. I will never forget it."

That gesture let everyone in the park and the world at large know that the captain of the Dodgers had accepted this African-American on the team. So everybody else in Dodger blue had better get on board as well.

Not to mention the rest of baseball.

Asked later why he did that, Pee Wee said simply, but firmly, "Because it was the right thing to do."

Jackie was capable of leading a team to victory in so many ways, whether it was with his bat, his legs, his glove, or his heart. But it took Pee Wee to find a way to make sure Jackie was accepted as a member of the team.

I wish Pee Wee hadn't left us after the 1959 season, his coaching career consisting of just one year. It was a big loss for baseball. And certainly a big loss for us.

Fortunately, we still had Campy. He duplicated the Campy's Bullpen of Vero Beach at the Coliseum and later at Dodger Stadium. He was usually at the games, available to offer his feedback, when asked, to one and all.

When he was still a player, Campy used to say, "You have to have a lot of little boy in you to play baseball."

He was sure right about that. I know every time we talked, I walked away with a smile on my face like a Little Leaguer who had just made the starting lineup.

I was never prouder to be a member of the Dodger organization than I was on May 7, 1959. Team owner Walter O'Malley, showing his respect and gratitude to Campy for his years of service to the club prior to his career-ending accident, and his continued involvement with the team although in a wheelchair, staged Roy Campanella Night at the Coliseum. A lot of players have been honored by their teams upon their retirement, but nobody has ever had a night like the one given Campy.

The Yankees agreed to be part of it, flying in to play us in an exhibition game, a fitting reminder of all those Dodger-Yankee World Series that Campy was an integral part of.

How did L.A. fans react? Even though he never played a game in Los Angeles, a crowd of 93,103 showed up for his night.

At the time, it was the largest crowd ever to watch two major league teams play. That figure was surpassed in 2008 when, in commemoration of the 50th anniversary of the Dodgers' arrival in Los Angeles, they returned to the Coliseum for an exhibition game against the Boston Red Sox that drew a crowd of 115,300.

The highlight of Campy's night, a moment that still brings a lump to my throat nearly 60 years later, occurred when Pee Wee wheeled Campy out onto a darkened Coliseum field, the lights turned out and replaced with thousands and thousands of flickering matches or lighters struck by the crowd.

When Campy thanked the sea of faces before him, the tears flowed.

What most people don't know are the logistics required to bring the two teams together for an unscheduled game on a Thursday in the middle of the season.

The Yankees played a night game in Kansas City on May 6 and flew to L.A. after the game. May 7 was an off day for them. The Dodgers played a day game in Milwaukee on May 6, and flew to San Francisco afterward for a four-game series against the Giants. On May 7, we played a day game in San Francisco, then had a police escort to the airport immediately afterward. When we landed back home, we had another police escort from the airport to the Coliseum.

After the game, the Yankees flew home and we had yet another police escort back to the airport to return to San Francisco for a night game the next day. We didn't get back to our San Francisco hotel until 2:30 or 3 in the morning.

We played four games in three cities in three days — two day games, and two night games. But, we didn't lose our focus, winning three of the four games against the Giants in that series.

And not one player complained about the inconvenience.

That's because the players, especially the guys from the Brooklyn days, remembered how Campy had always been there for them, a leader along with Pee Wee, a man who always seemed to say the right thing.

"After we won close games, the guys would celebrate in the clubhouse," said Duke. "In the midst of all the merriment, Campy would get everybody's attention by saying in a loud voice, 'Fellas, the team that won today ... is going to win again tomorrow.' The guys would cheer even louder. He had set the tone for the next game. Campy had a presence about him. You could be in the clubhouse with your back to the door and still sense that someone had just come in. When you turned around, there was Campy. There was something special about him."

Duke told me about one time at Ebbets Field when he didn't appreciate Campy's presence. That's because Campy was wearing his catching gear at the wrong time. The incident occurred in a game in which Duke was batting third and Campy fourth. With two outs in this particular inning, Duke was about to step into the batter's box when he noticed that Campy was wearing his shin guards and chest protector as he came out of the dugout. He walked into the on-deck circle, ready to go back behind the plate, obviously on the assumption that Duke was going to make the third out.

"Why do you have the equipment on?" Duke yelled out above the roar of the crowd. "Don't you think I can hit this pitcher?"

"No!" Campy yelled back. "That's why I put the equipment on."

Backing off from the plate, Duke said, "I'm not going to get in the batter's box until you take your gear off."

With a shrug, Campy did just that, tossing his gear back into the dugout.

A couple of pitches later, Duke hit a lazy fly ball into shallow center field for an easy out. Running down the first-base line while the ball was still in the air, he turned his head toward Campy and cussed out the Dodger catcher.

Campy started laughing as he hollered back, "I told you I didn't think you could hit that guy."

Campy wasn't immune to being on the receiving end of a laugh. One time that Brooklyn players loved to talk about occurred at now long-gone Forbes Field in Pittsburgh. It was Little League Day, and approximately 5,000 kids in uniform were parading around the warning track after batting practice.

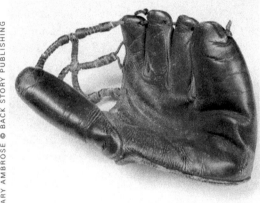

GARY AMBROSE © BACK STORY PUBLISHING

Duke Snider gave this glove to Ron as a keepsake. Snider used it for many years, but its open webbing later was deemed illegal.

Most of the Dodgers were in their dugout when a Little League team, wearing Dodger uniforms, walked by. Campy, sitting on the top step, saw a pudgy kid in the group and said, "Young man, what position do you play?"

"Campy, you're my favorite player," said the kid with a smile on his face, "and I'm a fat-ass catcher just like you are."

Campy's teammates roared with laughter, and stayed on him for days afterward.

Duke also knew how to have a few laughs on the field. One time, an umpire called a strike on him on a pitch he thought was too low. Duke put his bat on his shoulder and started to walk away.

"Where are you going?" asked the umpire. "That's only strike two."

"I'm going back to the dugout," Duke said. "If I have to hit that pitch, I'm going to need a 9-iron."

One umpire, Larry Goetz, got the best of Duke in a 1952 game at Ebbets Field against the Cincinnati Reds in which the Dodgers set a modern-day record by scoring 15 runs in the first inning. Duke hit a two-run homer on his first time up and then, in the same inning, walked in his second at-bat.

That inning just kept going and going, and soon, he was walking up for his third trip to the plate. There were two outs and the bases were loaded. The count went to three balls and two strikes.

The next pitch was a foot outside, but Goetz raised a fist to the sky and hollered, "Strike three! That's enough of that shit. If you can't win with 15 runs, you never will."

"The record," Duke insisted to me, "should be at least 16 first-inning runs."

There were more Duke Snider stories when the Dodgers came west. One didn't elicit any smiles in the Dodger front office.

During batting practice one day in the Coliseum, guys were debating whether anyone could throw a baseball over the left-field screen and then over the rim of the stadium, which was 143 feet above the playing field.

Don Zimmer bet some teammates that Duke could do it, and then told Duke his share of the winnings would be $200.

It was an offer Duke was happy to accept. He stretched, limbered up his arm, took a running start, and fired away. The first throw sailed easily over the screen, but rattled up against the last row of seats at the top of the rim. He wound up again, grimaced as he expended every bit of energy he could muster, sent the ball on its way in a high arc, and thought he had cleared the rim, only to see the ball hit the concrete wall just behind the last row of seats.

So close.

More determined than ever, Duke picked up a third ball and told Zimmer, "This last one is out of here."

But instead, as Duke cocked his arm back and began his forward motion, the ball slipped out of his fingers. Even worse, he heard a popping sound. He had dislocated his elbow.

Buzzie was not happy. He fined Duke $200. Plus, Duke lost his opportunity to win $200.

Undeterred by losing money and playing time, Duke got involved in another crazy challenge a few days later. This time, I was his partner in a two-man team, dumb and dumber. Our goal was to hit a golf ball from home plate over the right-field fence, over all the remaining grassy area to the end of the field, and then over the peristyle arches at the far end of the Coliseum.

Could it be done? We just had to find out. So, one early afternoon, before anyone had arrived for that night's game, Duke and I took our golf bags down to the field and started hitting golf balls. We were able to reach the peristyle arches, but could never get a ball over them.

Our fun ended when people started coming out of the offices inside the peristyle structure to see who or what was bombarding them. Who knew there were offices in there?

So, we came up with Plan B, hitting balls over the left-field screen, the seats behind it, then over the rim.

The next day, a member of the ground crew came to Duke and me with one of our golf balls that he had found and asked if we would sign it. We were happy to do so, although it's not easy to fit two autographs on a golf ball.

And yeah, that contest was stupid, too.

But for Duke, it all worked out in the end. On the last day of the season, figuring he'd have all winter to heal if he got injured again, he took one more shot at throwing a baseball over the rim and, this time, he cleared it.

Zimmer, agreeing that the offer was still good, paid Duke the $200. And Buzzie, with the season over, gave Duke back the $200 he had fined him.

Back when he was in Brooklyn, Duke wasn't trying to throw baseballs or hit golf balls out of the park. He was smashing home runs into the seats, hitting 40 or more in five straight seasons in the mid-1950s.

By the time he got to L.A., however, he was hampered by a bad knee and stuck in a stadium with a weird configuration that required any fly ball hit to right center or center field to travel between 425 and 440 feet to clear the fences.

It's a shame that the fans in Los Angeles, Duke's hometown, never got to see the player who was often compared to the center fielders of New York's two other teams of that era, Mantle on the Yankees and Willie Mays on the Giants.

I never tired of hearing Duke's stories about playing in Brooklyn, but, with an insatiable appetite for more memories about those colorful years, I also sought out every other member of our roster who had come west.

Right-hander Carl Erskine, who pitched for Brooklyn for a decade before finishing up his career with two final seasons in L.A., told me a story that illustrated how Brooklyn fans felt about their team.

Leaving for Ebbets Field one day, Carl was asked by his wife, Betty, to stop at their neighborhood grocery store on his way home to pick up a few items. When Carl went to the cash register to pay, the owner waved him off. "No, I can't take your money," he told Carl. "You play for the Dodgers and you shouldn't have to pay for your food."

The pitcher protested, but to no avail.

The next day, he went back to the market and insisted that the owner accept tickets for him and his family to attend a Dodgers game.

In 1948, Carl was pitching for the Fort Worth Cats, a Double-A Dodger farm team in the Texas League. He was doing well enough to get the attention of Branch Rickey, the parent club's president and general manager.

Rickey is best known for his monumental decision to sign Jackie Robinson to a Dodger contract. But like any human being, Rickey had his flaws. He was a very frugal person. Some described him as cheap.

For example, he communicated quite a bit by telegram because it cost less than long-distance telephone calls. And a man like Rickey, an innovator who created the minor league farm system, had a lot of people he needed to communicate with across the country in 1948 because the Dodgers had 26 minor league teams that year.

Bobby Bragan, the player/manager of the Fort Worth Cats, got a telegram from Rickey every day.

One of them read, "Can Carl Erskine help the Dodgers?"

Wanting to keep the reply short and inexpensive, Bragan sent back a one-word reply: "Yes."

By the time Rickey received the answer from Bragan, he had forgotten what the question was because he sent out so many telegrams. So he replied to Bragan, "Yes, what?"

Bragan, wanting to show deference to the man who was the most respected person in baseball at the time, sent a telegram back that read, "Yes, Sir."

In a half-century of baseball, I saw just about everything that could possibly happen on the field. But in a game in June 1959, I saw something I had never seen before or since.

We were in Philadelphia facing the Phillies at Connie Mack Stadium. Richie Ashburn was a great line drive hitter for Philly. He got a lot of hits, and sent a lot of foul balls into the seats.

In this particular game, Ashburn hit a liner over the Philadelphia dugout. It hit a fan with such force that the person required medical attention. There was a slight delay in the game while a stretcher was brought in.

Once the medical personnel reached the fan, play resumed. Back at the plate, Ashburn fouled off several more pitches.

By that point, the fan was on the stretcher and being carried through the stands toward the first-aid facility. When the next pitch was delivered, Ashburn fouled it off as well. Again he smacked a line drive and, believe it or not, *it hit the same fan*, this time just before the stretcher reached the exit tunnel.

Ashburn hit the same guy twice in the same at-bat. It was the double play from hell.

As the season moved along, we remained in contention for the pennant. But, after winning seven straight and nine out of 10, as June turned into July, we dropped three out of four.

Before the last of those losses, Pee Wee came up to me in St. Louis, reached into his pocket, and pulled out a pebble. It was about the size of a dime and very smooth.

"Keep this," he told me. "It will bring us good luck."

I put it in my windbreaker. I didn't think about that pebble for a long time after that because the weather was warming up and I seldom wore that windbreaker.

Immediately ahead of us was a four-game series in Chicago against the Cubs. Buzzie Bavasi was concerned enough about our slump to fly to Chicago, too antsy to sit home and listen to us lose on the radio.

Buzzie's flight didn't arrive in Chicago until late in the evening. Around 11 p.m., while walking to our hotel after eating dinner, he saw one of our pitchers going into a bar. Buzzie peeked in the door and saw two more Dodger pitchers behind the bar, mixing drinks and having a great time.

Buzzie knew they wouldn't make it back to their rooms before the midnight curfew. When he reached his room, he called the first player on the rooming list 15 minutes after curfew and got no answer. So he knew there were at least four of his guys out after curfew on a team that was on a losing streak and was facing back-to-back doubleheaders against the Cubs over the next two days.

He was pissed.

Buzzie didn't even check any other rooms. He was mad enough already.

The next day, we were about to take batting practice at Wrigley Field when Manager Walt Alston pulled the team off the field, telling us there was going to be a meeting in the clubhouse. Attendance was mandatory.

That didn't sound good.

We knew it wasn't good when we entered the small, cramped locker room and saw Buzzie. He did not look happy.

He reached into his coat pocket, pulled out an envelope, held it up for all to see, like a prosecutor producing a key piece of evidence in a courtroom, and said, "Last night, I checked everyone's room and I have the names here of everyone who was out after curfew. As you all well know, the fine for missing curfew without permission is $100. I want every one of you who missed curfew to walk into the trainer's room right now. If you don't come and your name is on this list, the fine will be 500 bucks."

It was decision time. Do we gamble that our names were not on that list and risk paying $500, or do we walk in and accept our $100 worth of punishment?

The trainer's room was even smaller than the clubhouse, with enough space for a whirlpool tub, a rubbing table, and not much else.

That room suddenly got a lot more cramped. Player after player marched in until there wasn't enough room for everybody.

Buzzie had a big smile on his face. His bluff had worked.

"OK," he said, "everybody go back to your lockers."

Once we were seated in front of our stalls, like school children being punished, Buzzie made an announcement. "If you guys don't win three of the four games in this series," he said, "it will cost everyone in this room $100."

The pressure was on. Yes, there was a pennant race going on, but all we could think of at the moment was that $100. We lost the first game, but won the nightcap of the doubleheader and swept the doubleheader the next day to move to within half a game of first place at the All-Star break.

In the clubhouse after the last game, you would have thought we had just won the pennant. The slump was over and no one was fined.

There were a lot of pressure games ahead as we moved into the second half of the season. We stayed close to the league lead most of the rest of the way, even briefly edging into first place for a day on three occasions, proving that we might just be capable of making the unprecedented leap from next-to-last to first in the eight-team National League.

Buzzie deserves a lot of credit for making that happen with roster moves that made him look like a genius.

During the previous winter, he had acquired outfielder Wally Moon in a trade with the Cardinals, and then picked up another Cardinal outfielder, Chuck Essegian, in a June trade.

Moon walked onto the field at the Coliseum, gazed at the left-field screen 251 feet away and smiled. He was a left-handed hitter not known for his power. He had averaged just under 16 home runs a season over his five years in the majors. There was no way he was going to be successful trying to aim for those distant right-field fences. But left field? Why not? So he worked on a swing that would enable him to loft pitches to the opposite field, loft them high enough to get over the 42-foot screen. The result was the Moon Shot, a series of home runs that enabled Moon to succeed where so many other left-handed hitters had failed, using the short distance to left to his advantage rather than putting himself at a disadvantage by allowing the vast acreage in right and center to gobble up his fly balls. In 1959, Moon hit 19 home runs and raised his batting average from .238 the previous season to .302.

In June, Buzzie called shortstop Maury Wills up from Triple-A Spokane. Maury was no kid. A journeyman, he had been in the minors for 8½ seasons. To his credit, he was still working on his game. A natural right-handed hitter, he was learning how to be a switch hitter. At first, Maury struggled playing short and had trouble hitting left-handed. In his first game as a Dodger, he made two errors, and in his first 12 at-bats for the club, he got just one hit.

Years later, I learned from Don Zimmer that Buzzie had told him that he had soon tired of watching Wills play and was going to send him back to the minors. Buzzie assured Zimmer that he was going to be the Dodger shortstop for the rest of the season.

But then Zimmer fouled a ball off his foot in batting practice and couldn't play for a couple of games. Wills was put back in the lineup. He began to hit, Alston kept him in the lineup, and Maury continued to improve. He learned to be more effective as a left-handed hitter by chopping down on the ball and using his speed to get on base, and, of course, also using that speed to steal bases. Soon, the job was his.

Buzzie also beefed up his pitching, calling up both Larry Sherry and Art Fowler from the minors. The 23-year-old Sherry could throw hard and had a great slider. Fowler was 36, but still had a very good fastball and was capable of being our closer.

Erskine was having arm problems and was considering retiring. He could still throw hard, but, between innings, his arm would stiffen up and he couldn't get it loose again. Buzzie plugged Roger Craig into Erskine's place in the starting rotation, but kept Carl on the team, using him in the bullpen.

People who thought we might fade and revert to the seventh-place team we had been the year before as the season wore on had it backward. We actually played better in the second half.

Our starting pitchers worked deeper into games and our veterans, like Duke, Gil, Carl, and Jim Gilliam, showed they could still produce at the plate. And all the moves Buzzie had made paid off. Moon continued to launch his Moon Shots, Wills became a solid shortstop, Craig won 11 games (2.06 ERA), and Sherry won seven (2.19).

With three games to go, we were tied for first with the defending champion Milwaukee Braves.

Our last three games were against the Cubs at Wrigley Field, right back where we had started the season. With the first game in extra innings, I flied out deep to center in the 11th.

With Hodges at bat, I went into the clubhouse to get a different glove. The radio was on in there and I could hear Cubs announcer Jack Brickhouse calling the game. I can still hear that broadcast in my mind, Jack saying, "If we get Gil Hodges out here in the 11th , I know the Cubs will score in their half of the inning and beat the Dodgers. Here's the 3-1 pitch to Hodges …"

And then an instant of dead air followed by one word uttered by Brickhouse: "Gone." He didn't say "a long drive to left" or "back, back, back." Nothing but "Gone."

Gil had the hit the ball over the bleachers, then across the street, and into a tree. It traveled at least 450 feet.

We won, 5-4, and Milwaukee lost, but then we got clobbered, 12-2, the next day. We both won our final game to finish tied, forcing a best-of-three playoff series for the right to face the Chicago White Sox in the World Series.

We won the first game of the playoffs, 3-2, in Milwaukee, Sherry beating Carlton Willey. The Braves scored two runs in the second inning, but Sherry, in relief, shut them out the rest of the way.

Playing the second game at the Coliseum, we were down 5-2 in the ninth, but scored three times to tie the game up and then, in the 12th, with Hodges on second and two out, Carl Furillo hit a bouncer over the mound and over second base that was fielded by Milwaukee shortstop Felix Mantilla on the other side of the bag. But his off-balance, desperate throw to first was in the dirt and got by first baseman Frank Torre. The ball bounced off the shoulder of Dodger first-base coach Greg Mulleavy as Hodges came home with the pennant-clinching run.

From the press box, announcer Vin Scully uttered the words that echoed all over Los Angeles that day and was replayed for years, "… Hodges scores, we go to Chicago."

So, we went to Chicago, where I played in my first World Series just a year after playing in the College World Series. It was such a special pair of seasons for me.

Chicago's team was referred to as the Go-Go Sox because they were a lot like our club — lots of speed along with great defense, quality pitching, and a few sluggers.

The pitching staff was led by Early Wynn, a 22-game winner. Their top power hitter was Ted Kluszewski.

The World Series opened in Chicago with their impact players leading them to victory. Living up to his name, Wynn won early, beating us in Game 1 with Kluszewski hitting two home runs. We got our asses kicked, 11-0.

We got on the team bus quietly and slumped in our seats for the ride back to the hotel. Quietly, that is, until Zimmer got on board. Standing at the front of the bus, he said in a loud voice, "Who the fuck are the Go-Go White Sox?" Everybody on the bus broke out laughing.

With a sarcastic line, he had eased the tension and got us to focus on the game ahead, not the disastrous one we had just played.

When the bus arrived at the hotel, four or five players and their wives went to the bar for a cocktail before going out to dinner. Soon, more players joined the group, and the booze flowed. When the bill came, it was for around $350, without the tip. In 1959, that seemed like a lot more money than it would today.

As we struggled to figure out who owed what, Sandy Koufax grabbed the bill, added a tip, and signed it, "Walter O'Malley."

The next day, most of the players were in the lobby waiting to go to the ballpark when Mr. O'Malley, our owner, dropped by to wish us well in the game ahead.

Then, he added, "I hope everyone enjoyed themselves yesterday in the lounge after the game. However, I would appreciate it very much if you wouldn't do that again. Good luck."

We thanked him, knowing that he was expecting us to pay him back with four victories. We made a down payment that day at Comiskey Park with a 4-3 win in Game 2.

That game started out looking like Game 1 with the White Sox scoring two runs in the first inning. Sitting there frustrated, I stuck my hands in my windbreaker and felt something. It was the pebble Pee Wee had given me months earlier. I rubbed it and, sure enough, we came back and won.

I should probably mention a few other factors that also helped. We tied the series by using an aspect of our game that we were not known for — power. All of our runs came via home runs, two by Charlie Neal to drive in three and the other by Chuck Essegian. Johnny Podres did what he was known for, pitching well in clutch situations where a win was crucial. Johnny pitched six innings to get the win, and Sherry pitched the final three for the save.

Then it was back home to the Coliseum for three straight games. The Dodgers had expected huge support from their new fans when they arrived in L.A. in 1958 and had their optimism validated when 78,672 showed up for the home opener. But now, with the Dodgers amazing the baseball world by leaping from seventh to a pennant in just their second year in L.A., the team's

Ron shows off the good-luck pebble given to him in 1959 by Pee Wee Reese. Pee Wee said it would help the Dodgers, who moved from next-to-last to World Series champs in only one year.

popularity soared even higher. In each of the three games, the Dodgers set a new World Series attendance record — 92,394 in Game 3, 92,650 in Game 4, and 92,706 in Game 5. Those numbers might never be exceeded.

In Game 3, Furillo broke a scoreless tie in the seventh with a two-run single, and that was all we needed in a 3-1 victory.

In Game 4, Wynn was back on the mound. We got our revenge on him, scoring four runs in the third. Chicago tied us with four in the seventh, but Hodges homered to left in the eighth to give us a 5-4 victory.

With a chance to wrap up the series in Game 5 in front of the largest crowd to ever watch a World Series game, we failed. Koufax was the losing pitcher, although he allowed only one run in seven innings, a run that scored while we were completing a double play in the fourth. But that's all the White Sox needed for the 1-0 victory.

Back in Chicago with a second chance to clinch the series, we didn't blow the opportunity again. We raced out to an 8-0 lead by the time we were done batting in the fourth, and won, 9-3, with Snider, Moon, and Essegian all hitting home runs. Sherry, relieving Podres with one out in the fourth, made sure the Go-Go Sox were gone by shutting them out the rest of the way.

Sherry won two games, had saves in the other two Dodger victories, and was named the MVP of the World Series.

The Dodgers had been playing in Brooklyn since 1890. In 67 years, they won one world championship. We had equaled that in two seasons in L.A.

For Mr. O'Malley, that bar tab was a bargain.

Of course, I know why we really won. It was because of that lucky pebble Pee Wee had given me.

I still have it today, in the windbreaker hanging in my closet.

# 8

## The Duke Comes Home, the Dodgers Come Apart

I DIDN'T HAVE MUCH TIME to celebrate our triumph over the White Sox in the World Series. There was a military obligation waiting for me. Three days after the final out in Chicago, I had to report to Ford Ord, California, for six months of active duty in the Army.

Eight weeks of basic training was a lot tougher than eight weeks of spring training. And then, instead of having a season to look forward to, I was shipped to Fort Gordon, Georgia, outside of Augusta, where I was assigned to the military police.

Hard to believe I was living the good life at the top of the baseball world just a couple of months earlier. Now I was in Georgia in one of that state's coldest winters in 25 years, and my platoon leader, Sgt. Manning, was a diehard White Sox fan.

He decided to get even with me for the Dodgers beating his team. Every time he needed volunteers, I was chosen. He would say, "I need three volunteers to … no, I need two volunteers for a detail. Cactus Jack, you're the third one."

Why he called me Cactus Jack, I have no idea, but he worked me hard.

But then, one afternoon shortly before my discharge, Sgt. Manning told me, "Cactus Jack, you just volunteered to go with me." We got into a jeep and off we went. We came to a residential area, he got out, and said to follow him. We turned a corner around a building, and there was a barbecue going on.

As an office grunt fulfilling his Army reserve obligation in 1962, Ron was overloaded with paperwork by his Dodgers teammates Don Drysdale, left, and Sandy Koufax.

Sgt. Manning turned to me and said, "How would you like a beer?" There was no detail. He brought me along to hang out with a couple of his buddies and get something to eat and drink. It was my going-away present. We had a great time.

But he had to keep up his image. He took me back to my company, and when he dropped me off, he said, "If you tell anybody about today, the next time we are at the shooting range, I will shoot you in the ass."

The sergeant was tough, but he turned out to be a good guy.

By the time I was discharged, spring training was over. No fishing for me that year.

And no spot on the Dodgers. I was shipped to Spokane, a Triple-A farm club. We had a heck of a team there with a starting outfield consisting of Frank Howard, Willie Davis, and me, although Frank was soon called up by the Dodgers.

Even the best of teams can have a slump, and we experienced one midway through season. It seemed like we were just going through the motions and not playing with much enthusiasm.

Fortunately, we had a great manager in Preston Gomez, masterful at handling young players. He called a team meeting to remind us of what was at stake, not only for the team, but for each of us individually.

"I want you guys to look around the room," he said, "and tell me how many teammates you see who have the ability to make it to the major leagues. And don't count yourself."

As we all looked around the room, Preston continued.

"I probably see more potential major league players than you all do," he said. "I see guys who have exceptional talent and ability. But what I haven't seen lately from a few of you is the extra effort and desire needed to get to the majors.

"Here's something for you all to think about. As your manager, I fill out a scouting report on each player in this room every week and send it to the Dodgers front office. In the report, I tell them what I see. That has a lot to do with what the Dodgers decide to do with you at the end of the season. They can call you up, trade you, or send you back to the minors. It's up to you. My next report is due in five days.

"Gentlemen, enjoy the rest of the evening."

Our attitude and enthusiasm improved rapidly and remained high for the rest of the season. We went on to have a great year. Willie Davis set the Pacific Coast League record for triples with 26, and I hit .303 with 27 home runs and 100 runs batted in. We won the Pacific Coast League championship by 11½ games, averaging nearly 5½ runs per game.

I rejoined the Dodgers at the end of that season, appearing in only 14 games at the big league level.

I was back on the big league roster in 1961 and never returned to the minors, partly because of a suggestion made two years earlier by Charlie Dressen, one of our coaches. In spring training of 1959, he told me to get a first baseman's glove. "The more positions you can play, the better your chance of making the team," he said.

I got the same model of glove Gil Hodges used. Might as well copy from the best. The Dodgers had two first basemen in 1959, Gil and Norm Larker. Sometimes, neither of them wanted to take infield practice, so they asked me if I would fill in for them. I was happy to do so. I had always been an outfielder, but I thought of Dressen's advice.

He was right. With right-hander Jack Sanford starting for the Giants against us in a June game in San Francisco, Walt Alston wanted another left-handed hitter in the lineup. Before the game, he asked me if I had ever played first base before. No, I told him.

"Well," he said, "you're playing there today."

With 40,000 fans in attendance at Candlestick Park, I was nervous standing in the field in such an unfamiliar spot. Infield practice was one thing, but game action was quite another.

In the first inning, I got my first touch on the receiving end of a perfect throw from Maury Wills to complete a double play.

When I got to the dugout, Roger Craig, our starting pitcher that day, complimented me. I had to laugh because the reality is, I didn't have much of a choice. If I hadn't caught that ball, it would have hit me in the chest.

The real confidence booster for me came in the second when I got my first ground ball and handled it easily, throwing to Maury for a force-out at second.

After the game, Walt told me I had done well. I felt comfortable at first, and I knew he felt comfortable enough to put me there when needed, increasing my value to the team and my playing time.

To bolster our pitching staff in 1961, Buzzie made a trade that brought us Turk Farrell, a veteran right-hander with a mean streak.

One night in Cincinnati, we lost a close game to the Reds, and Farrell, upset about the defeat, had a few drinks after the game.

There are happy drinkers and there are some not-so-happy drinkers. Farrell was in the second group. While walking back to the hotel, he broke the antennas on every parked car he passed on the street.

Buzzie, with us on that trip, was walking behind Farrell, watching. Buzzie pulled out a pen, wrote down the license plate of every damaged car and, over the next few days, working with the motor vehicles department, contacted the owners and paid for the repairs.

Then, he did some damage to Farrell's paycheck, deducting the cost of the new antennas.

Farrell later blamed his actions on the pressure he felt being on our club. "I don't like pitching for the Dodgers," he said, "because every time I go out there, it may mean the pennant."

Buzzie relieved the pressure after the season by leaving Farrell exposed for the expansion draft, enabling the Houston Colt .45s to sign him.

He wound up facing us at Dodger Stadium, and it soon became obvious he hadn't been taking any anger-management classes.

He was losing, 6-1, in the fifth inning, not only because of our offense, but because of his team's defense as well. The Colt .45s had made four errors by the middle of the fifth, one of them by Farrell on an attempted pickoff of Wills at first.

Unable to take it anymore, Farrell snapped. Unfortunately, it happened with me at bat. On the first pitch, he stuck a 99 mph fastball in my ribs. The space between your hip bone and your rib cage is roughly the size of the ball, and that's exactly where he got me. I had a lump in my side for over a month.

After that, every time I faced Farrell, I wanted to hit a line drive off his kneecap and watch him roll on the ground. I guess I had a little mean streak, too. At least that's the way I felt then, but, over time, you tend to mellow out and forget those feelings.

Then again, maybe you don't.

We won 89 games in 1961, but finished second, four games behind Cincinnati. The Reds deserved to win. We had a solid team, but were disappointed because we didn't play well at the end.

That left a bitter taste in our mouths as we headed into winter, but the memory hardened our resolve to make up for it with a pennant in 1962.

When we reported to Vero Beach, spring training was a little more serious, although that did not stop our guys from having fun. We played golf, fished, and the usual suspects stayed out late a few times.

Midway through camp, the team took its annual trip to Miami. Duke Snider and I had a room next to one of our pitchers.

One night, Duke and I were in our room around 9 or 10, watching television, when there was a knock on the door connecting the two rooms.

I opened it, and there was the pitcher standing in his underwear. One look told me that he had obviously had too much to drink. Standing behind him was a violin player wearing a tuxedo, and behind him was a hooker getting undressed.

The pitcher asked if we could take care of his valuables. He handed me his wallet, watch, and money clip, and told me he'd get them in the morning. I took the valuables, nodded, and shut our side of the door.

Duke and I soon heard the sound of the violin. The music was pleasant and romantic, but it only lasted a few minutes. Then, silence.

We watched television for a while until Duke said, "I think we should check to see if he's OK."

Quietly, we unlocked the door, poked our heads in, and saw the pitcher on the floor, passed out. We craned our necks around the door to see inside the room. The violin player was in bed with the hooker.

The major leagues expanded in 1962, and the National League added the New York Mets and the Houston Colt .45s.

The Mets lost an all-time record 120 games that first season under the leadership of the one of the great characters in baseball history, Casey Stengel, nicknamed "The Old Perfessor."

When his players struggled, Casey had no qualms about taking vocal jabs at them. He referred to his catcher, Choo-Choo Coleman, as the best in the league at fielding passed balls.

The most memorable member of that team was "Marvelous" Marv Throneberry. He was a decent hitter, but a poor fielder best known for an unforgettable trip around the bases.

It occurred one afternoon at the Polo Grounds in a game against the Cubs. With the Mets already trailing, 4-1, in the first inning, Throneberry came up to bat with two runners on base and drove a ball into the gap in right center, good for a triple and two RBIs.

Or so it would seem. But remember, these were the '62 Mets.

The first baseman asked for the ball on an appeal play, claiming Throneberry hadn't touched first base. The first baseman stepped on the bag, and the umpire signaled that Throneberry was out.

Casey charged out of his dugout to protest the call. But the first-base coach, Cookie Lavagetto, stood in his path.

"Don't bother, Case," Lavagetto said. "He didn't touch second, either."

In anticipation of Throneberry's birthday that season, an order was placed with a bakery for a cake. The team acknowledged his birthday but didn't give him the cake.

After the game, a sportswriter asked Casey what happened to it.

"The cake looked great," he said, "but we didn't want to risk having Marv drop it."

Center fielder Richie Ashburn, a future Hall of Famer, was on that team as was Elio Chacón, a shortstop from Venezuela who spoke very little English.

Two or three times during the season, Ashburn and Chacón collided going after a short fly ball.

Finally, Mets right fielder Joe Christopher, who was bilingual, suggested that the outfielders communicate with Chacón in Spanish.

"How do we say, 'I got it,' in Spanish?" asked Ashburn.

"Yo la tengo," said Christopher.

"OK, if I holler, 'Yo la tengo. Yo la tengo,' that means, 'I got it. I got it,' and you get out of the way. Got it?" Ashburn told Chacón.

"Sí," said Chacón.

A few days later, when a short fly ball was hit into left center, Ashburn came running in as Chacón went back for it. Ashburn hollered, "Yo la tengo! Yo la tengo!" and Chacón peeled off, getting out of Ashburn's path.

He was about to catch the ball when left fielder Frank Thomas crashed into him, knocking him on his butt as the ball bounced away.

When Ashburn got back on his feet, he said to Thomas, "Didn't you hear me call for it?"

"What the hell does 'yellow tango' mean?" said Thomas.

In 1984, an indie rock band formed in Hoboken, New Jersey, and went on to success that has lasted more than three decades. They called themselves Yo La Tengo in tribute to the always entertaining 1962 Mets.

The Old Perfessor, who was 72 that season, would often shut his eyes for a minute or two in the dugout during games to catch a quick snooze. When he awoke, he would jump up and holler, "Run, sheep, run!" Nobody knew exactly what that meant, but his players figured it had something to do with players running the bases.

Don Zimmer, who played on that team, had some fun with Casey one afternoon.

"It was a day game in the Polo Grounds," Zimmer told me, "a warm afternoon and not much was going on in the game. When Casey shut his eyes for a minute, I whistled real loud and yelled, 'OK, let's go.' "

Casey woke up startled, jumped to his feet, and hollered, "Run, sheep, run!" The guys on the bench had a good laugh — it was between innings, and nobody was running anywhere.

When the Dodgers left Brooklyn after the 1957 season, the move to the West Coast made a lot of baseball fans in L.A. happy, but it upset the entire borough. Brooklyn was a very diverse community, and what kept the city together was the bond people shared as Dodger fans.

Fans felt betrayed by Walter O'Malley when he moved his team to Los Angeles. They called him all sorts of nasty names.

When the Mets were formed, they chose colors reminiscent of the teams they had lost, blue for the Dodgers and orange for the Giants.

So when the Dodgers returned to New York in 1962, the first time the team had returned to its ancestral home, I was curious to see how the fans would react.

Media coverage was huge and fan interest was intense.

Our first appearance on the Polo Grounds field would be for a double-header. Duke Snider and I left early for the stadium. When we arrived, there were about 5,000 fans waiting for us just outside the entrance. I have never seen that large a reception committee in my entire career.

When the team bus arrived an hour or so later, there weren't many familiar faces on it from the Brooklyn Dodgers. Most of those guys had retired or been traded. Gone were Reese, Furillo, Erskine, and Newcombe. Hodges was on the Mets, and Labine had briefly been with them for a couple of weeks at the start of the season. Jackie Robinson had retired years earlier, and Campy was in a wheelchair.

The fans booed me and every Dodger who hadn't played in Brooklyn when we came down the steps from the clubhouse, which was located in center field.

Attendance that day was 55,704, biggest crowd the Mets would draw in their two seasons at the Polo Grounds. There were around 45,000 people in their seats two hours before the first pitch.

I hurried out because I wanted to be on the field to see the reception for Duke. I was standing in shallow center field when he came out. The fans knew Duke's No. 4. When they saw it, they began to cheer.

He briefly stopped in center to say hello to Ashburn, then continued slowly walking toward our dugout. The applause for Duke never stopped. The closer he got to the dugout, the louder those hands clapped. It was the longest applause I have ever witnessed, lasting 15 minutes, well after he had stepped down into the dugout.

The visiting teams were given 30 minutes to hit in batting practice; the guys who were not in the starting lineup got only five minutes. Duke was in the latter group that day. Normally, the nonstarters took five swings the first time around, then one or two swings apiece the next round, depending on how much time remained.

Duke was the second player to step into the batting cage. He didn't hit the first three or four pitches worth a damn. Then BAM, the ball flew into the seats and the crowd went crazy. It sounded like he had just hit a home run to win the World Series.

Duke started to get out of the cage to give the next hitter his turn, but everybody told him to stay right where he was, and to keep swinging.

Duke took the balance of the five minutes and put on a hitting exhibition. With a few seconds remaining, he launched a ball into the upper deck.

When he came out of the cage and jogged around the bases, he got a standing ovation. I've never seen anything like that for a player in batting practice.

Carroll Beringer, who had thrown batting practice, came into the dugout, "I've never been that nervous in my life," he admitted. "I couldn't get the ball over the plate. It took me a few pitches before I could give Duke anything good to hit."

When the game started, the fans began chanting, "We want Duke! We want Duke!" The chant went on without interruption every time the Dodgers were at bat over the entire doubleheader.

We had a 12-4 lead at the end of eight innings, and I was due up in the ninth. With the fans still chanting, "We want Duke," I asked Alston if he would let Duke hit for me in the ninth, but he said, "No, I want you in right field for defense." It was the only time in my career I asked to be taken out of a game.

When I did get up to the plate, I was showered with one of the loudest boos I had ever heard. The fans wanted Duke. They didn't get him, nor a victory in that game or the second game. Duke didn't play in that one, either.

After the doubleheader, he took me to a couple of his favorite hangouts to have a drink. When we asked for the check at one place, a bartender came over and said, "Welcome back to New York, Duke. You'll never pay for a drink while I'm tending bar."

The next day, Duke and I were walking to lunch when a cab pulled up alongside us. The cabby honked his horn and, with a heavy New York accent, yelled out, "Hey, Duke, good to see ya. Welcome back to New York," then drove off.

The following day, we passed a homeless guy lying on the sidewalk. When he looked up and saw Duke, he pulled himself up to a standing position, smiled, and said, "Duke, where are you going? Duke, you're my hero. Do you remember the day you hit two home runs against the Pirates? I was there."

He followed us down the street for another block, talking baseball all the way, then wished Duke, "Good luck."

The Dodgers may have left Brooklyn, but some Brooklynites never left the Dodgers.

Here's the sad thing about that series. We beat the Mets in all three games, but Duke did not appear in any of them, despite the ever-present chants. When the series was over, Duke told me how badly he had wanted to play. To this day, I don't know why Alston didn't let him hit for me in the ninth inning of that first game, considering that we had an eight-run lead and Sandy Koufax was still going to be pitching in the bottom of the ninth.

In the 1950s, no player hit more home runs (326) or drove in more runs (1,031) than Duke Snider. He appeared in seven World Series, eight All-Star Games, hit 407 home runs, drove in 1,333 runs, and, in 1980, was inducted into the Hall of Fame. Yet for all of that, I feel he was an underrated player, never receiving the full recognition he deserved.

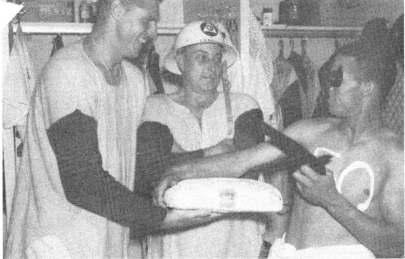

Maury Wills, right, heists a base in the clubhouse from Dodgers teammates Frank Howard, left, and Johnny Podres in 1962. Wills set the major league record for stolen bases that year, with 104.

As the 1962 season wore on, it became clear that a member of our team, Maury Wills, was on a record-breaking path. He wound up racing past Ty Cobb's single-season stolen base record of 96 by getting 104. Maury received a lot of publicity for that feat, deservedly so.

But Jim Gilliam, the man who paved the way to second or third for his illustrious teammate on many occasions, should have been given more credit for helping Maury. Batting behind him in the No. 2 spot, Gilliam spent much of the season batting with two strikes on him. Time and again, he wouldn't swing at good pitches in order to give Maury more opportunities to steal.

Gilliam was the epitome of a team player, doing so many little things that never make the headlines, but win games.

For example, when I played first base and Gilliam played second, he let me know when off-speed pitches were coming to left-handed batters. The second baseman can see the signs a catcher calls, signs that are out of the line of sight of the first baseman. When the pitcher started his windup, if an off-speed pitch was coming, Gilliam would say, "Ronnie" loud enough for me to hear but out of earshot of the batter or the first-base coach. That pitch would make it more likely that the ball would be coming in my direction. Gilliam's vocal tip prepared me. It was a simple signal that could have a big impact.

He had a great feel for the game, anticipated situations with unerring accuracy, was streetwise, and a very good pool player.

We had several different affectionate names for him. Junior was one because that was part of his actual name. That turned into June Bug.

My favorite was Devil. During spring training one year, Junior went into a pool hall just outside of Vero Beach, reached into his pocket, pulled out a wad of bills, dropped them on the table, and said, "Who wants the Devil?"

Everyone in the pool hall thought about it, then put their sticks back in the rack. Nobody wanted any part of him. After that, we all called him Devil.

Junior was one of those guys I always enjoyed being around. I wish he was still around today.

I found it interesting how players remembered details of games played years earlier. I was batting in the eighth inning of a tie game between us and the Milwaukee Braves at the Coliseum with right-hander Don Mc-Mahon on the mound. There were two outs and the bases were loaded.

As I walked from the on-deck circle toward the batter's box, I looked back and saw Hodges and Snider in the dugout, and Reese in the third-base coaching box all cheering for me to get a hit. It's always a good feeling to have teammates pulling for you, but these three guys made it a special at-bat. So special that I remember it to this day.

McMahon was a power pitcher who didn't have a good curveball but did have one of the best sliders in the league. After working the count to 3-1, I thought, "OK, here comes his slider in on my hands. Get ready for it and hit it hard somewhere."

I took a quick glance at Reese and saw that he was giving me the take sign.

Take? Really? Every batter in the world loves to hit with a 3-1 count, but I couldn't swing because I had the damn take sign.

The next pitch was, indeed, a hard slider right on my hands. Grudgingly, I took the pitch and the umpire called ball four.

It was so close that it could have been called a strike and I would not have argued.

The runner from third scored with what proved to be the winning run.

The next day, McMahon, obviously annoyed, came up to me during batting practice and asked, "Why didn't you swing at that pitch last night?"

I told him that I had the take sign.

"Bullshit," he replied. "They wouldn't give you the take sign in that situation. Why didn't you swing?"

Again, I said a little more emphatically, "I had the take sign."

"Bullshit, bullshit, bullshit," said McMahon, walking away, shaking his head.

Ten years later, I bumped into him at a USC football game and he said to me, "I still don't believe you had the take sign that night."

The pitch bothered him that much.

The Giants had a relief pitcher named Stu Miller. No one would ever describe Miller as a power pitcher, but, with one of the best change-ups in the game, he made power hitters look terrible at the plate. At times, it was embarrassing to see how feeble he made good hitters look. In one horrendous streak for us, he struck Frank Howard out six straight times.

"The way to hit Miller," Hodges once said, "is to wait until the instant he releases a pitch, look down at your feet, count to three, then look up and hit the ball."

Gil was kidding, but the basic concept of having the patience of a fisherman when dealing with Miller was sound.

One night before a game against the Giants, Walt, in a pregame meeting, told us, "Stu Miller can't blacken your eye with his fastball, so get on top of the plate and wait for the slow stuff."

That night, our catcher, Norm Sherry, followed Alston's instructions, explicitly. He crowded the plate, and Miller hit him with a fastball and broke his wrist.

The next day, one of our players said, "Maybe Miller can't blacken your eye, but he can break your wrist."

Pregame meetings can be very serious, but I remember a moment in one of them that still gives me a laugh all these years later.

We were going over the opposing hitters and Alston brought up the name of a left-handed hitter who had just been called up from the minors. "Does anyone know anything about him?" Walt asked.

One of our players was familiar with the hitter because he, too, had just been called up. Anxious to contribute, he said, "I do."

"OK, what can you tell us about him?"

"I played against him all year long," said our young player. "He's married, has two kids, and drives a station wagon."

I f we were playing a night game and had a day game the following day in another city, Alston and Bavasi would often send the starting pitcher for the day game ahead on an afternoon commercial flight. That way, at least one of us would be well-rested for the game, as the rest of us might not get into that city until the wee hours of the morning.

On one occasion, we had a night game in Cincinnati, so pitcher Stan Williams was flown to Chicago for our game the following afternoon against the Cubs. Because we wound up playing extra innings game in Cincinnati, we didn't check into our hotel in Chicago until 2 a.m.

As we stood at the front desk getting our keys, here came Stan, casually walking into the lobby after a night on the town.

If we had played a normal nine-inning game, we would have beaten him to the rooms.

Fortunately for Stan, he pitched well that day, and we beat the Cubs.

That was Stan, always confident enough to live on the edge. And somehow, it worked for him.

One exhibition season, he was part of a Dodger squad sent down to Cuba to play a few games. Alston sent his pitching coach, Joe Becker, along to manage the team. So they were named Becker's Bastards.

At night, some of the guys would go to the Havana casinos to gamble. On the final day of the trip, Stan was down to his last 50 bucks. Sitting at the blackjack table, he bet all of it on one hand. Dealt a nine and a three, Stan put both hands over his cards as if he was praying and said, "Lord, please give me an eight," then told the dealer to hit him. Sure enough, the card was an eight.

"Shit, if I had known that," said Stan, "I would have asked for a nine."

ANDY CAREY

Tommy Davis also had a banner year in 1962. On his way to 153 runs batted in, he and Dodgers teammates Stan Williams, John Roseboro, and Ron Fairly celebrate his centennial run.

Fortunately for him, the dealer was sitting on 16, and had to hit as well. He drew a four, so the hand ended in a push.

Stan, figuring he had used up his allotment of divine intervention, got up, put his 50 bucks in his pocket, and walked away.

Stan even outsmarted our front office when it came to making money. He threw as hard as anyone in the league, but had control problems. As an incentive to solve that problem, the Dodgers put a clause in his contract that if he had no more than a certain number of walks that season, he would receive a $500 bonus. It seemed like a good idea.

But the Dodgers soon detected a pattern Stan had devised to guarantee himself the bonus. When he had three balls and no strikes on a hitter, he would simply hit the batter intentionally. There was nothing in his contract about that.

"There was no way I could throw three strikes in a row," said Stan, "so, I just stuck one in the batter's ribs."

That clause only lasted a year.

After another spectacular outing in 1962, Sandy Koufax blows a clubhouse kiss to Don Drysdale, far right, as Frank Howard, left, and Tommy Davis also pay respects.

ANDY CAREY

We had a superlative offense in 1962 led by Tommy Davis. He hit 27 home runs, had a league-leading .346 batting average, and drove in 153 runs to set a Dodger single-season RBI record that remains unbroken to this day.

I remember one stretch when I was hitting behind Tommy and he was on such a hot streak that I didn't hit with a runner in scoring position for two or three weeks. He had driven in everybody.

That season, Tommy knocked in a run once every 4.34 at-bats. In getting 230 hits, he had 68 multi-hit games, 26 three-hit games, and six four-hit games.

I kidded the run-producers who usually hit ahead of me in the lineup (Frank Howard and Willie Davis, along with Tommy): "Before I came to the plate, you guys hit 79 home runs and drove in 357 runs. You didn't leave anyone on base for me."

We won 101 games in 1962, but, unfortunately, so did the Giants to tie us at the end of the regular season.

Injuries are never an excuse, because every team has them. That said,

I have to mention that Koufax was limited in the second half of that season by a circulation problem on his pitching hand. Normally, when someone presses a finger down on a flat surface and then lifts it up, the finger turns from white back to red as the blood rushes back. When Sandy did that with his left index finger, the redness didn't fully return. And that finger was always cold.

Sandy had a crushed artery in the palm of his left hand caused by an at-bat in which an inside pitch jammed the knob of the bat into the palm. The injury forced him to miss two months of the season. He returned just 10 days before the postseason.

As a result, Sandy made only 26 starts in 1962, around 15 fewer than he had when he was injury-free. He wound up 14-7. I have to believe that, had he been at full strength, he would have won at least one more game.

And that's all we would have needed.

In those days, the postseason consisted of only one series — the World Series. But because we were tied with the Giants, we had to play a best-of-three series to determine the pennant winner who would face the American League champs, the Yankees, in the World Series.

Game 1, played in San Francisco, was won by the Giants, 8-0, with left-hander Billy Pierce throwing a complete-game shutout.

We won Game 2 back home in Dodger Stadium, 8-7. The game was decided in the bottom of the ninth when I came up with Wills on third. Staring out at me from the mound was Mike McCormick, my traveling companion back when we were both star high-school players taken to New York for the Hearst Sandlot Classic.

Now we were rivals with the pennant on the line. I was able to get enough wood on a pitch to hit a fly ball to center. Willie Mays caught it, but Wills scored from third on the sacrifice fly to win the game, and set up a deciding third game.

Playing at home, we fell behind, 2-0, but went ahead, 3-2, on a two-run homer by Tommy Davis, then added another run when Wills got his 104th stolen base at third, then scoring on the subsequent wild throw by catcher Ed Bailey.

Going into the ninth, we led, 4-2, three outs from a pennant.

Matty Alou led off the inning for the Giants with a single to right.

The next batter, Harvey Kuenn, hit a perfect double-play ball to Wills at short, but Larry Burright, our second baseman, was playing closer to first base than to second. By the time Burright hustled back to the second base, he was just able to handle Wills' throw to get a force-out, but didn't have enough time to complete a double play.

Instead of two outs and no one on base, there was one out with a runner at first. Give a major league team an extra out and anything can happen. In this case, something did happen, and it was disastrous for the Dodgers.

After Willie McCovey and Felipe Alou walked to load the bases, Mays lined a ball off the glove of pitcher Ed Roebuck for an infield hit that scored a run. Orlando Cepeda then got the tying run home on a sacrifice fly. After the Giants loaded the bases again, Stan Williams walked in the go-ahead run, and another came home on an error by Burright on a ground ball. San Francisco had rallied to get four runs on just two hits with four walks, an error, and a wild pitch. Our pitching and defense completely fell apart. We gave the Giants five outs in what was the worst inning we played all year.

With Pierce on the mound, we went quietly in the bottom of the ninth without getting a man on base. We lost, 6-4.

Going into the ninth inning, bottles of Champagne were on ice just outside the Dodger clubhouse waiting to be popped. When San Francisco rallied in the ninth, the Champagne was rushed to the other side.

Afterward, the walls of the Giants clubhouse, splashed with the bubbly, echoed the hooting and hollering of a wild celebration, but there was only silence next door in our clubhouse. Most of us just sat in our locker stalls, still in our uniforms, staring at the floor, replaying the game in our minds, pinpointing the moments when it got away.

It was my most disappointing afternoon in Dodger blue.

Two questions still haunt many of us to this day. One, why had bench coach Leo Durocher moved Burright away from his normal position at second? Kuenn had hit a perfect one-hopper to Wills. If he had not been forced to wait for Burright to get back to the bag, it would have been an easy double play.

Two, Drysdale, a 25-game winner that season, was warming up in the bullpen in the ninth, and was ready to come in. After McCovey walked, we should have brought Don in to pitch to Felipe Alou and Mays. But Walt didn't want to use Don because he wanted him to pitch in the first game of the World Series.

The pitcher for the National League pennant winner in the World Series opener was Billy O'Dell. I know because I watched it on TV.

# 9

## Blood on the Diamond:
## Big D and the Brushback Wars

BEANBALLS HAVE BEEN a part of baseball as long as fastballs. Cal McLish, who pitched in the majors for 15 years, then became a pitching coach, used to tell young players, "Pitchers are concerned about three things — velocity, movement of the ball, and the location of the pitch. Hitters have three things to think about, too. They can take the pitch, swing at it, or duck."

In baseball today, you're not allowed to intentionally knock the batters down, and that's good. Players have multiyear contracts and are paid so much money that throwing at a player doesn't belong in the game.

Today, if a pitch comes close to a hitter, many of them want to fight.

Years ago, it was a matter of survival. Because the knockdown pitch was commonplace, a pitcher who wanted to keep his job had to use it on occasion.

It might be to send a message to a hitter who had shown up the pitcher. It might be in retaliation for a knockdown pitch fired at a teammate. It might be to back off a hitter who crowded the plate. Or, sometimes, it might be to test a hitter's mental toughness. If the knockdown pitch seemed to affect a batter, he could be assured of seeing a lot more of them. So we all knew, if we get knocked down, we must not show our emotions. Just get up, step back in the batter's box, and hit the next pitch hard somewhere between the foul lines, showing the pitcher that the knockdown pitch had no effect on our mind or resolve.

The best at doing that in my era was Frank Robinson. When we faced him, our pitchers were told, "Don't knock him down. You'll just piss him off, and then there's no telling how many runs he'll knock in."

If, however, we knew a hitter was affected by the knockdown pitch, our pitchers would brush that hitter back a couple of times in the first game of a series. After that, he didn't do much at the plate.

When it comes to knockdown pitchers, two stand out in my mind — Drysdale and Bob Gibson. I don't know who was more intimidating. Pick your poison.

I played with a couple of guys who got the "24-hour flu" the day they were scheduled to face Drysdale or Gibson. Both were very competitive and hated to lose.

Big D, as Drysdale was known, used to say, "You can beat me ... but you're not going to enjoy it as much as you think you are." He would also say, "If you hit the batter hard enough, he won't charge the mound."

It was not pleasant to face Don. He stood 6 feet 6 inches, weighed 210 pounds, and was a hard-throwing right-hander with a three-quarter delivery.

He had an amazing career. In 14 seasons, all with the Dodgers, Don appeared in 518 games, had a record of 209-166, an ERA of 2.95, and 2,486 strikeouts. In 1968, he set the all-time record for consecutive scoreless innings at 58 $2/3$, a record later broken by another Dodger, Orel Hershiser, who had 59 consecutive scoreless innings. Don had several great years, but his best season was 1962, when he was 25-9 and won the Cy Young Award.

Over his career, he averaged 245 innings a season. He retired in 1969 because of a torn rotator cuff, well before pitch counts became a key factor in determining how many innings a starting pitcher would be allowed to work.

I wouldn't want to have been the manager who had to tell Don he had thrown 100 pitches and was done. He probably would have thrown a 101st ... at my head.

Don hit 154 batters in his career and menaced all who faced him. It is from that aspect of his performances on the mound that so many stories have come.

Soon after Don joined the Brooklyn Dodgers in 1956, the team purchased the contract of right-hander Sal Maglie from the Cleveland Indians. Maglie was known for throwing pitches a little too close to hitters and hence the nickname "The Barber." After learning how to pitch under Maglie's tutelage, Don took that approach to the next level because he threw harder than Maglie.

We loved Don as a teammate because he always had our backs.

Literally.

"You swing as hard as you want," he would tell us, "and I'll protect you. If opposing pitchers throw at you, they will only do it once."

That's the way we felt on the rare occasions in batting practice when we got a taste of what opposing hitters faced by hitting against Don. We would have preferred to have done it only once.

He hated to throw batting practice because he felt he had to accommodate the hitters' preferences rather than working on his own repertoire.

"Why is it called batting practice?" he once told me. "Why can't it be called pitching practice?"

Back then, pitchers didn't have a protective screen in front of them during batting practice. It was felt that with no protection, pitchers could practice reacting to balls hit back at them. That was a stupid idea. Whoever thought of it was definitely not a pitcher.

There were no complaints from Carl Furillo, who used the setup to practice one of his favorite tactics. "If you hit the ball hard enough to get it by the pitcher," he said, "you have a better chance of getting a hit. It's the biggest hole in the infield."

Remember, it was Furillo's bouncer over the mound against Milwaukee that clinched the 1959 pennant for us.

Unfortunately, Carl also hit several pitchers with line drives in batting practice. Guys like him led to the invention of the pitching screen.

Don disliked throwing batting practice, and in spring training, he didn't like pitching anywhere but Vero Beach. So when he couldn't pitch at home because of a rainstorm and was told by Walt Alston that he would have to fly to St. Petersburg to throw batting practice, Don wasn't happy. When the plane encountered thunderstorms, bounced around, and made a rough landing, Don, who didn't like to fly in the best of conditions, had soured on the assignment even more by the time he took the mound.

Pitching at Al Lang Field, Don first faced Duke Snider who hit a line drive that just whizzed past the mound. Two pitches later, Duke whacked a ball that was so close to Don that he had to duck to get out of the way.

Now, he was really pissed.

For his next swing, Duke asked for a change-up. When Don threw it, Duke hit a hard ground ball at Don's feet that forced him to jump in the air to avoid getting hit. He came crashing down on the mound, tearing a hole in his pants and spiking himself on his knee. As Don pulled himself up, there was blood on his pants.

All of our teammates who had been watching roared with laughter. That made Don even madder.

"Get your ass back in there," he shouted at Duke.

No way, Duke told him. Although Don kept yelling at him, Duke just smiled and walked away.

When the next batter got in the cage, Don threw the first pitch under the hitter's chin, knocking him on his ass.

Alston walked hurriedly out to the mound. Don told him, "You can take this shooting gallery shit and shove it up your ass. Now it's my turn to have some fun."

Alston stuck his hand out and told Don in his no-nonsense manner, "Give me the ball. That's enough for today."

Don's workout had lasted nine or 10 pitches. It's the only time I have seen or heard of a manager making a pitching change during batting practice.

Even when he wasn't mad, you really had to concentrate when Don threw batting practice. You couldn't just get in the cage and swing because, unlike other batting practice pitchers, Don moved the ball around in the strike zone and changed speeds. If he threw a pitch low and away and you hit it hard the other way, he had a tendency to throw the next pitch even harder in on your hands. He loved to jam hitters and break their bats, then laugh like hell at them.

One spring, we were taking batting practice at our home field in Vero Beach, Holman Stadium, and Don was pitching BP. Holman was a big ballpark and not many home runs were hit there. It was 360 feet down the lines and 440 feet to straight away center. It didn't have fences, but there was a 9-foot embankment with a kumquat tree on top of the upward slope.

When it was my turn to hit, I figured, after seeing a few pitches, Don was going to try to jam me, so I was looking for a fastball inside. Sure enough, there it was, and I got all of it. I hit the ball over the kumquat tree in right field and jumped out of the cage. As I was running to first base, I heard Don holler at me, "You've got two more swings." I hollered back, "I don't want them. You can have them," and laughed at him.

A few days later, he was throwing batting practice again. I'd forgotten about what had happened a few days earlier, but not Don. A pitch came whizzing at me up and in. Way in.

Down I went. Don had flipped me on my ass.

When I got up, I was pissed. "You SOB," I yelled at him. "What was that for?"

"Ah hell, Ron," said Don, laughing as he spoke, "you're going to get knocked down during the season. I thought you might want to practice that, too. Are you OK?"

I called him a few more dirty names, and all he did was laugh. We had dinner a couple of nights later and Don said he was sorry, that he was trying to come inside, but didn't mean to knock me down.

I appreciated his apology and, after having seen that ball zeroing in on me, was glad I didn't have to face him in a game. When he threw inside against an opposing hitter, he had no regrets, and was never sorry.

In a game against the Pirates in Pittsburgh, we had a narrow lead, but the Pirates had the tying run on second with two outs and Donn Clendenon, on a hitting tear, due up next. With first base open, Alston went to the mound and told Don, "Put Clendenon on and go after the next hitter."

By the time Alston reached the top step of the dugout, Don had already started his windup.

The pitch hit Clendenon in the ribs. He went to first base, Don retired the next batter, and the inning was over.

As soon as Don reached the dugout, Alston said to him, "I thought I told you to walk Clendenon."

"No," Don told him, "you said to put him on. I don't need four pitches to do that. I can get him there in one. Besides, it may help the next time he hits."

The two faced each other one more time in the game. Don threw him three sweeping curveballs away, and Clendenon took three feeble swings, striking out.

A catcher named John Bateman got drilled in the ribs by Don when Bateman was with Houston. Eight years later, he and I were on the Montreal Expos, and Don was one of the team's announcers.

One day in spring training, the Expos' batting practice pitcher was experiencing arm problems. Don, who would occasionally help Manager Gene Mauch in the spring by putting on a uniform and serving as an extra coach, agreed to step in and finish throwing to the last few hitters.

We all got seven swings. When Bateman stepped in, he took three very weak swings, and stepped out of the cage. I asked him why he wasn't taking his remaining swings.

"I know Drysdale is trying to lay the ball in there to hit," Bateman said. "I can see that we're wearing the same uniform, but I'm not comfortable and I don't trust him. Besides, four more swings are not that important in my life."

Don was so intimidating that even when the sting of one of his pitches had faded, the emotional scar could still remain, in this case, even eight years later.

He could be especially intimidating to batters if they thought he couldn't see them. That was the case in the opening game of a series against the Cubs in Chicago.

When the Dodgers arrived in town early on the night before the game, Don, even though he was pitching the next day, went out to dinner with the Cubs' Don Zimmer, his old Dodger teammate. They met at a popular cocktail lounge near Wrigley Field. After dinner, they had a drink that led to another and another. They stayed there drinking so long that it was dawn by the time they left.

They had a day game in front of them, so they decided to go straight to the ballpark. When Zimmer got to the Cub clubhouse, he spread the word that he had been out all night with that day's starting pitcher for the Dodgers.

"Drysdale is drunk," Zimmer said.

Not really. Don could hold his liquor as well as anyone on the team.

As the two teams took the field for batting practice, word got back to Don that, thanks to Zimmer, the Cubs were licking their lips at the idea that they'd be feasting on balls thrown by a pitcher struggling under the influence of alcohol.

In the bottom of the first inning, facing Chicago's leadoff hitter, Drysdale went into his act, turning his body away from the plate and toward the on-deck hitter, squinting in that direction in search of the catcher's signs.

Johnny Roseboro, in on the joke, stood up behind the plate, whistled in Drysdale's direction and hollered, "Over here!" Don backed off the mound, then turned toward home plate and threw the first pitch as hard as he could, the ball sailing over the head of the batter and smashing against the screen behind home plate.

"Shit," said one of the players in the Chicago dugout, "he's throwing that hard, but can't see where the ball is going?"

When third baseman Ron Santo, one of Drysdale's close friends, came to the plate, he yelled, "Hey, Don, can you see me?"

"I could knock a couple of their hitters down," said Don, "and they couldn't get mad at me because Zimmer told them I was drunk."

Drysdale wound up getting a complete-game victory and striking out 10, the Dodgers winning 8-1.

Heck of a job for a "drunk" pitcher.

After the game, Drysdale called Zimmer in the Cub clubhouse and asked if he wanted to have dinner that night. Zimmer told Drysdale that he never wanted to see him again.

That didn't last long.

On another trip to Chicago, we heard rumors that the Cubs were stealing signs.

Bob Buhl pitched for them in the first game of the series. The next day, about the second or third inning, one of our players noticed this guy sitting in the bleachers in right center wearing a trench coat. Very suspicious. I can't remember ever seeing a Chicago bleacher fan wearing a trench coat. It was Buhl. Then, we noticed he had binoculars and held a scorecard up to his chest on fastballs, but not on curves.

So we sent Lee Scott, our traveling secretary, out to talk to Buhl. All Lee said was, "Bob, you don't have to sit here. I have a couple of tickets we are not using today, and they're right behind home plate."

Message sent, message received. It was the last time we saw any of their pitchers in the bleachers.

Drysdale was scheduled to pitch the day after we caught Buhl. Even though he wasn't in the bleachers anymore, we still didn't want to take any chances, so, we changed the signs.

Don called every pitch with his feet. If he stood on the mound with one foot on the rubber, it was a fastball; two feet on the rubber, it was a curve. For his change-up, he moved his right foot left and right on the rubber, then took his normal stance, leaned in, and pretended to be getting the signs from Roseboro who could put down any combination of fingers because none of those signs meant anything.

One evening at Dodger Stadium, Don was having a tough night. The home plate umpire sensing that Don's frustration was about to boil over, walked out to the mound and told him, "Don't throw at the next hitter because, if you do, it will cost you 50 bucks. Get behind the plate," Don told the ump. "I have a whole bunch of $50 bills in my pocket."

Sure enough, Don brushed the next hitter back and, yes, he was fined $50.

It was Sandy Koufax, not Don, who was on the mound in Candlestick Park when Juan Marichal's shocking, ugly attack on John Roseboro occurred in 1965. But it was a war of words between Marichal and Drysdale that kindled the fiery confrontation.

The rivalry between the Dodgers and the Giants goes back to the decades when both teams were in New York. Today, the rivalry between the Yankees and the Red Sox is considered the bitterest in baseball. But in terms of longevity and drama, Dodgers-Giants has it beat.

The feelings of hostility between the two teams remained just as intense when they moved to California.

The Giants were our arch enemies. I didn't like their ballpark, I didn't like their uniforms, and I didn't like them.

Both sides were always on edge when we faced each other, but early that season, the rancor seemed even more heightened than usual, if that was possible. That's because the number of knockdown pitches thrown by both sides at each other had escalated.

Marichal singled out Drysdale as the instigator, saying that Don had far exceeded the acceptable limit on targeted pitches, having hit Willie Mays, Orlando Cepeda, and other Giants. It had to stop, Marichal said, or he would do something about it. If Drysdale is pitching against me, Marichal insisted, and he comes close to anyone on my team, I'll hit him good. I vow to protect my players.

As expected, Don didn't back down. Instead, he threw wood on the fire, saying that he was only 60 feet 6 inches away on the mound, that Marichal knew where to find him, and that if Juan wanted to come after him, he would be happy to meet him halfway.

National League President Warren Giles jumped in, issuing a warning, saying that any pitcher who intentionally threw at a hitter would be heavily fined.

In late August, we went to San Francisco for a weekend series against the Giants. The teams were yapping at each other in the first three games, the animosity evident. But it was just talk.

On Sunday, however, in the final game of the series, the words of warning turned out to be more than an idle threat as the anger bubbled over.

Even before the game started, I could feel something was in the air, and it wasn't good.

We had Koufax on the mound and they had Marichal. Maury Wills led off the game with a single and scored on my double in the first inning.

The next time Maury came to the plate, Marichal knocked him down with an inside pitch. When Willie Mays came up, Sandy answered in kind, throwing a pitch over Mays' head. That showed how much the rage was mushrooming, as it was extremely rare for Koufax to get involved in a knock-down war.

Marichal had no interest in cooling the situation down. When I came to the plate for the second time, he knocked me down.

What was going to happen when Marichal himself came to the plate?

All hell broke loose.

Sandy threw a pitch inside that backed Marichal off the plate, but Sandy wasn't head hunting. The pitch was close enough to the plate almost to be a strike.

But when Roseboro threw the ball back to Koufax, he fired it close to the side of Marichal's head. The Giant pitcher later claimed that it nicked his ear. Marichal thought Roseboro was trying to hit him in the head. Expletives were exchanged between Marichal and Roseboro.

The next thing I saw was surreal, something I had never seen before or since — a hitter attacking the catcher with his bat, using it as a weapon.

As Marichal struck Roseboro in the head, Sandy came running down from the mound and tried to disarm the Giants pitcher.

Both teams rushed onto the field and the fight was on.

Cepeda came out of the San Francisco dugout with a bat in his hand. Danny Ozark, our third-base coach, confronted him. Ozark was big and a lot stronger than he looked. He had been in the Battle of the Bulge during World War II, so he was not afraid of a little fist fight.

"If you don't put that bat down right now," Ozark told Cepeda, "I'll shove it up your ass." Cepeda wisely dropped the bat.

Like in most baseball fights, the majority of the players were trying to break up individual fights and separate the combatants.

Two of the Giants, Mays and Len Gabrielson, did a particularly effective job helping to restore peace.

When things finally settled down, we finished the game.

After the final out, I went into our trainer's room to check on Roseboro. He was sitting on a rubbing table with eight stitches in his head.

"The security guard asked if he could get anything for me," Roseboro told me about the moment he walked in with blood on his head, "and I said, 'yes, bring Marichal in here, then get out and lock the door.' "

After the season, Roseboro told me a story that shocked me. A group of guys had come to see him when he returned home from San Francisco. "Give us the word," they told him, "and we'll shoot Marichal when he comes out of his hotel on the Giants' next trip to L.A."

"No," Roseboro implored them, "you can't do that. That is not right. Please, don't do it."

He made a passionate plea for them to respect his wishes and repeated it several times before they finally backed down.

The incident left a black mark on baseball, but it would have been 10 times worse had those guys acted on their impulse.

Time heals. It did with Roseboro and Marichal, who settled their differences and became good friends. That's a good thing.

But I'll never forget the frightening sight of Marichal swinging that bat in anger.

The memory of that horrifying moment was still fresh in my mind the next time we played the Giants. I knew Don would still be thinking about it as well, so I saw an opportunity to get to him by getting him riled up the way he got to me by knocking me down in batting practice.

Don was scheduled to start against Marichal, so when we were out the night before, I brought up the gruesome attack on Roseboro and reminded Don what he had said about protecting his players.

"Marichal will probably knock us down," I told him, setting off the fuse, "and you won't do a thing about it."

That definitely ignited Don's temper. He started talking about what he would do if Marichal started head hunting. "If he knocks down any of our hitters," he said, "I'll knock down two of theirs."

I had gotten Don so fired up, that responding verbally wasn't enough. As he spoke, he punctuated every word with his left index finger, poking me in the chest.

He was really prodding hard, with that look in his eye that he would get when he was about to throw a fastball with bad intentions, but I refused to flinch.

The next morning when I got up, I saw seven or eight black dots on my bare chest. If I had a magnifying glass, I probably could have seen Don's fingerprint.

When I got to the ballpark, I found Don at his locker rubbing his index finger. When he spotted me, he started hollering at me.

I just laughed, knowing I had finally gotten to him.

Fortunately, it wasn't the index finger on his pitching hand. That would not have been funny. But once Don got to the mound, I could see that, every time he caught the ball with his glove, he winced.

I think it just made him meaner because he wound up pitching well, and winning.

Don didn't always need a fastball to jab somebody — he could also use a verbal jab to get someone's attention.

During the season, roommates took turns tipping the bellman when they brought luggage up to the room. We generally tipped them four or five bucks.

In the early 1960s, Don roomed with outfielder Lee Walls. When the bellman brought their luggage to the room, Walls would say, "Don, take care of the bellman. All I have are $100 bills."

Initially, Don just shrugged, and reached in his wallet. But it got a little old after it happened too many times.

So, on one road trip, he came prepared with change for a $100 bill. At the first hotel, the bellman brought their luggage to the room and, sure enough, Walls looked at Don and said, "Get the bellman, roomie. All I have are hundreds."

Don smiled and replied, "Give me one. I have change."

Don took the bill from Walls, gave the bellman 40 bucks, and handed 60 back to Walls.

After that, Walls always had money for the bellman.

Nobody took our crushing loss to the Giants in the 1962 playoff series harder than Don. It had been his best season personally. He led the majors in wins (25), strikeouts (232), and won the Cy Young Award. And yet, it was all for naught. Again, he would watch the World Series on television.

Like the rest of us, he spent a long winter agonizing over what might have been. As competitive as he was, I know that ninth-inning collapse that resulted in the come-from-ahead loss gnawed at him.

But when he and I and the rest of our club came back to Vero Beach for spring training in 1963, I think we had put all the shoulda, woulda, coulda thoughts behind us, and were totally focused on getting another shot at the World Series.

For me, the first loss of the season came before Opening Day, and it was really tough emotionally. On April 1, we were in Albuquerque for an exhibition game when I heard the Dodgers had sold one of our players to the Mets: Duke Snider.

Wait a minute, it was April Fools' Day. So, this was a joke, right?

No, it was for real. Duke, bothered by knee problems, had played in only about half our games the previous season, hitting just five home runs with 30 RBIs. And this was a chance to close out his career where it had all started, playing in New York before the fans who so adored him.

Still, it was a sad day for me. He was more than just a teammate. He was the Duke of Flatbush, the last of the Boys of Summer, and he was our captain. I lost my roommate, my hitting coach, and the companionship of a close friend. He gave me and everyone on the team confidence just seeing him in his uniform. Even though we knew his best days were behind him, we were like a bunch of kids thinking, "We can beat you guys because we have Duke on our team."

I really missed my friend from that day forward, and even more so after he passed away in 2011 at the age of 84.

After we had traded Stan Williams to the Yankees in the offseason for Bill Skowron, management decided to pair up Skowron and Frank Howard as roommates. A couple of us were sitting around having a beer one day, and someone asked why those two had been matched up. "Because," said Drysdale, "they didn't want to fuck up two rooms."

One morning in Chicago, it was raining and our game was postponed. Around noon, some of us decided to go to the movies. Skowron, whose nickname was Moose, said he wanted to ask his roommate to join us.

Whenever Skowron called anyone on the phone, he identified himself by stretching his name out, saying, "M-o-o-o-se." Everybody who knew Skowron knew whose voice that was.

Everybody except Frank. While we waited in the hotel lobby, Skowron went to a house phone, called his room and, when Frank answered, said, "It's M-o-o-o-o-se."

"I'm sorry, he's not here," said Frank, who then hung up.

I could probably fill a book with just Frank Howard stories. Here's one more.

We were playing in Wrigley Field on a bright, sunny day. The Cubs got two runners on with two outs. When a fly ball was hit deep to right, Frank, playing out there, chased it all the way back to the wall, brushing up against the ivy. He flipped his sunglasses down and seemed poised to catch the ball when a fan dumped a large bag of popcorn down on his head. Frank dropped the ball and two runs scored.

Alston immediately came out of the dugout to protest, claiming fan interference. When he got into an argument, Augie Donatelli, the ump, decided to hear the point of view of the man with the best view. He called Frank in from right field and asked, "Did that popcorn bother you?"

With a blank look on his face, Frank said, "What popcorn?"

Alston turned and walked back to the dugout, shaking his head all the way.

He got mad all over again the next day when he picked up the sports section of the Chicago Tribune and saw a front-page photo of Frank standing next to the ivy with popcorn raining down on him.

N ot counting the playoff game in which we beat the Giants in 1962, we won 101 games that season. In 1963, we won 99, but won the pennant by six games. It was a team built on outstanding pitching and solid defense.

We had a primary four-man starting rotation consisting of Koufax (25-5), Drysdale (19-17), Podres (14-12), and Bob Miller (10-8).

Here's how they performed in key categories:

- Games Started: Drysdale 42, Koufax 40, Podres 34, Miller 23
- Complete Games: Koufax 20, Drysdale 17, Podres 10, Miller 2
- Innings Pitched: Drysdale 315.1, Koufax 311, Podres 198.1, Miller 187
- Earned Run Average: Koufax 1.88, Drysdale 2.63, Miller 2.89, Podres 3.54
- Strikeouts: Koufax 306, Drysdale 251, Podres 134, Miller 125.

Looking at Sandy's numbers, the question many players had was, how did he lose five games?

Koufax and Drysdale had 37 complete games between them. Add Podres, and the total is 47. In 2016, the total number of complete games *in the entire National League*, for all 15 teams, was 39. The difference in philosophy concerning starters and relievers is the biggest change in the game in the last half-century.

Today, if a pitcher goes six innings and allows three runs or fewer, he is credited with a "quality start." That's an earned run average of 4.50.

Once asked what his definition of a quality start was, Sandy replied, "When the starting pitcher shakes the hand of the catcher after the game is over."

The excellent pitching wasn't limited to just the four main starters. The staff ERA that season was 2.85. That included a bullpen led by Ron Perranoski (16-3, 21 saves, 1.67 ERA).

Add it all up and it's no wonder that we went on to sweep the Yankees in the World Series.

# *10*

## The Golden Arm

WHAT CAN I SAY ABOUT Sandy Koufax that has not been said or written? Not very much. At least not about what he did on the mound.

But I knew the other Sandy, the one who was my teammate for nine years, giving me the opportunity to get to know Sandy the person and form a friendship that I will always treasure.

Sandy, who was from Brooklyn, got a tryout at Ebbets Field in 1954. After seeing his fastball, Al Campanis, then a Dodger scout and the man who arranged the tryout, told The New York Times, "The hair raised up on my arms."

At the end of the tryout, Campanis asked Dodger backup catcher Rube Walker, who caught Sandy that day, what he thought of the pitcher. Don't let him leave the park without signing him, Walker told Campanis.

The Dodgers signed Sandy for a total of $20,000 for 1955 — a $14,000 bonus, and a $6,000 salary.

At that time, any player who received a bonus in excess of $4,000 had to remain on the 25-man roster for two years. No minor league experience for them. The rule was designed to prevent rich teams from signing the best young players in the country, then storing them in their farm system. In reality, it also meant those teams had only 24 players they could depend on. Very few young players came out of high school or college ready to play in the majors.

And under this rule, sometimes they weren't ready for years. The best way to hone a player's natural talent is to have him play every day.

In Sandy's first two seasons with the Dodgers, he won four games and lost six, appearing in just 28 games and pitching a total of $100\frac{1}{3}$ innings. The bonus rule hurt young players like him. He didn't begin to realize his full potential until 1961. That season, Sandy's record was 18-13, with a 3.52 ERA. He pitched $255\frac{2}{3}$ innings, and led the league in strikeouts with 269.

What he did from 1961 through 1966 put him in the Hall of Fame. Combining his best three seasons — 1963, '65, and '66 — his record was 78-22, with a 1.88 ERA and 1,005 strikeouts.

Of those three years, I think 1965 was Sandy's best. He struck out 382 batters and walked 71, a difference of 311. Only one other pitcher in baseball history, Randy Johnson, has had 300 more strikeouts than walks in a season, but he wound up 10 behind Sandy, getting 372 strikeouts while allowing 71 walks for the Arizona

ANDY CAREY

Sandy Koufax, the winning pitcher, and Ron, who drove in the winning run, congratulate each other in the tunnel at Dodger Stadium after a game in 1962.

Diamondbacks in 2001, a difference of 301.

Speaking of differences, people often ask me to compare hitting off Koufax versus Drysdale. Both were great pitchers, fierce competitors, and both had great arms. The big difference was that Don was not a lot of fun to hit against because he was known for knocking hitters on their ass. Sandy didn't do that. You just couldn't hit him. It didn't make any difference what sign the catcher put down. Fastball or curve, it was the best in the league. Don didn't have a fastball or a curve to match those in Sandy's arsenal, but he had a very good spitter, and was more of a ground ball pitcher. While Don wasn't shy about throwing knockdown pitches, Sandy preferred to give a warning if he thought a Dodger had been hit or even knocked down on purpose.

If so, when the first batter on the opposing team came to the plate to start the next inning, Sandy would throw a fastball 3 feet over the head of the hitter. It was so far over that the batter would have had to jump high into the air to reach it. It was Sandy's way of saying, "That's enough, stop throwing at my hitters or I'll throw the next one lower." That approach instantly settled the issue.

The only time I ever saw Sandy show any emotion and throw at a hitter was in St. Louis, and the target was Lou Brock.

Sandy didn't get upset when a hitter got a base hit or even a home run. He got mad at himself for making a bad pitch. What did get to him was an opposing player trying to show him up or embarrass him.

In this game, Brock got on base, faked like he was going to steal a couple of times, then did steal second. He did the same thing once he had reached second, dancing around, daring Sandy to throw, then, on a subsequent pitch, stealing third. He started doing the same thing down the third-base line, dancing and daring, indicating a steal of home was next.

Brock never got that far because Sandy struck out the batter to end the inning.

The next time Brock came to the plate, Sandy didn't bother with a warning. He hit Brock in the back with a fastball.

Years later, when I played for the Cardinals, Brock told me, "Koufax got me good and I couldn't lift my right arm for a few days."

Whenever a game was close, the count was 2-2 or 3-2, and Sandy needed a strikeout, he had a routine. He would go behind the mound, grab the rosin bag, wipe the sweat off his forehead, step back on top of the mound, tug on his jersey, adjust his cap, take a deep breath, get the sign from the catcher, go into that trademark windup, and BAM, strike three.

He had just thrown a fastball with a little extra on it. The hitter didn't have a chance. Sandy's normal fastball was in the high 90s, but those clutch, third-strike fastballs were four or five mph faster.

He could do that to even the best of them. I'll never forget a test of skill between Sandy and Roberto Clemente in old Forbes Field in Pittsburgh. We had a one-run lead going into the bottom of the ninth, but the Pirates had a runner on first with two outs when Clemente came to the plate.

The count went to two balls and two strikes. Sandy threw Clemente three straight fastballs, and the future Hall of Famer hit each one foul down the right-field line, the last two far enough to have been a home run in fair territory. It appeared that Clemente was beginning to zero in on Sandy's fastball.

So, he moved behind the mound and went through his routine. He got back on the rubber, and Clemente, having seen a barrage of fastballs, figured another one was coming.

He was right, but that didn't help. Sandy reached back and put a little extra on it, and BAM! The pitch, in on Clemente's hands, was by him before he could swing the bat.

Called strike three, game over. "I don't know how he does it," John Roseboro told me in the clubhouse afterward. A lot of pitchers can add one or two miles an hour on their fastball, but Sandy adds five or six on his. He's the only one who can do that.

With Sandy on the mound in St. Louis one time, the Cardinals got a couple of runners in scoring position with two outs. Their pitcher, due up, was called back, and a pinch hitter was sent in. Before he got out of the dugout, he was told emphatically to look for Sandy's fastball. He went quickly — strike one, strike two, strike three. The hitter didn't swing at a single pitch.

Shaking his head, he trudged back to the dugout, where he explained, "You guys told me to look for Koufax's fastball. I just saw three of the damnedest curveballs I've ever seen."

Sandy's fellow pitchers on the Dodger staff were as much in awe of him as were opposing hitters. That's not always a good thing, as Pete Richert could attest.

It's understandable that a relief pitcher, sitting in the bullpen on a night Sandy was pitching, might assume that he was not going to have to leave his seat. Especially if he was the long man, whose job is to enter the game in the early innings if the starting pitcher is struggling.

That was 23-year-old Richert's role in 1963.

On the chalkboard:
Dodgers - 5
Mets — 0
No-Hitter
June 30, 1962
Koufax
(0 for 4)

**After a stellar performance on the mound, clubhouse pranksters made sure Sandy Koufax also remembered his performance in the batter's box.**

Often after night games, players go out for a sandwich or an adult beverage. Richert decided that if he wanted to have a drink or two, he would do so the night before Koufax was scheduled to pitch. After all, what are the chances that Sandy was going to get knocked out of the game in the first three or four innings? Slim and none.

So Richert had a couple of cocktails the night before Sandy was starting a day game.

It was a hot day at Dodger Stadium with the temperature in the high 90s. Sandy struggled in the first inning and was in trouble again in the second. Richert had warmed up twice when Sandy gave up an RBI single in the third.

Walt Alston came out of the dugout and walked slowly to the mound, trying to give Richert a little extra time to get ready.

"How do you feel?" Alston asked Sandy when he reached the mound.

"Better than the guy you have warming up," said Sandy, knowing where Richert had been the night before.

What could Alston say? Nothing, as it turned out. He just walked back to the dugout, Sandy went back to pitching, we scored some runs, and Sandy got the victory.

Lesson for a young reliever: Even if the best pitcher of his generation is on the mound, the only nights off you are guaranteed are those on the schedule.

One night, our scheduled starter, Claude Osteen, and Sandy were in a pregame meeting going over the opposing hitters. In discussing one particular hitter, Claude said, "I'm going to throw him breaking balls, then sink the fastball low and away to get him to hit the ball on the ground."

"You can also throw him fastballs in on his hands," said Koufax, trying to be helpful.

"Sandy," said Claude, "with your fastball, you can pitch the entire world in on their hands. When I need that fastball, you come out and throw it. I'm going to sink the ball low and away."

In 1963, Sandy decided to add to his repertoire by developing a third pitch, a slider. He worked on it in the bullpen until he thought it was good enough to try in a game.

"I'll try it on [Hank] Aaron," he said. "If it works on him, it will work on anybody."

The next time we faced the Milwaukee Braves, Sandy decided to test his new pitch in the first inning when Aaron came up. Swinging at the slider, he hit a 400-foot line drive down the left-field line foul by about 10 feet.

Aaron then turned to Roseboro, our catcher, and said, "Tell Sandy he doesn't need that pitch."

When Roseboro repeated Aaron's words to Sandy, he replied, "If Hank says I don't need that pitch, then I don't need it."

That may have been the only slider Sandy ever threw in a game.

On Sept. 9, 1965, we played the Cubs at Dodger Stadium with Sandy going against Bob Hendley, another left-hander.

The innings wore on, and the excitement grew in the stadium and around L.A. as word spread that Sandy was going not only for his fourth no-hitter in as many years, but also his first perfect game.

In just about every no-hit attempt, the pitcher tends to tire in the final three innings, losing a little off his fastball. That was not the case with Sandy that night, or in most of his starts. In many of his games, he threw harder in the seventh, eighth, and ninth innings than he did in the first three or four.

Before we took the field in the eighth, Jim Gilliam reminded the other infielders that Sandy had something special going, so "get in front of any ball hit to you and block it."

As it turned out, there was no pressure. No ball was hit to any of us after Jim's reminder. Sandy made sure of that. In the eighth inning, he struck out Ron Santo, Ernie Banks, and Byron Browne. In the ninth, he struck out Chris Krug, Joey Amalfitano, and Harvey Kuenn to complete the perfect game, the only one in Dodgers history.

He had finished strong, striking out seven of the last nine. Sandy retired more batters than the guys in the field. He had 14 strikeouts and we had 13 putouts.

Before the game, one of the Cubs had demonstrated to the entire team how, in his opinion, Sandy tipped his pitches. When the game was over, Santo told his teammate, who had claimed he had Sandy figured out, to stand on one of the tables in the center of the clubhouse and do his demonstration again so all his teammates could once more see how Sandy tipped his pitches.

"We knew what was coming," said future Hall of Famer Billy Williams, "and we still couldn't hit him."

Sandy threw his first no-hitter against the Mets in 1962. Sandy threw four no-hitters. Nolan Ryan later almost doubled the record by throwing seven no-hitters.

That September of 1965, the Giants caught fire, winning 14 straight games, and 17 of 18, threatening to run away with a pennant that had been tightly contested a little more than a week earlier. We had gone from leading San Francisco by one to trailing by 4½ in just 10 days.

One of the Giants had been quoted as saying, "We've chased the Dodgers all year long. Now, let them chase us for a while."

That comment was repeated so many times in our clubhouse that no one could possibly forget it.

I don't know if that remark was the fuel that fired up our team, but we suddenly got hot just as the Giants flamed out. We won 13 straight, and 15 of the remaining 16 games. In the last dozen games, we were 11-1, while San Francisco was 5-7.

We won the pennant by two games, clinching at Dodger Stadium on a Saturday, the next-to-last day of the season. The celebration was typical of those wonderful moments when the pressure of an incredibly tense race ends in triumph, and a lull settles in before the tension rises again with the first pitch of the World Series.

As the last bottle of Champagne was drained, the final bottle of beer slam-dunked into a trash can, Alston found me in the mass of drenched ballplayers to let me know that I was not going to be in the lineup for the final, meaningless game the following day against the Milwaukee Braves. It would be a day off for me.

So when Drysdale invited me to join a group of the guys at a San Fernando Valley restaurant to continue the celebration, I figured I didn't have to worry about how late I'd be out.

It was late when I got home, but I couldn't go to bed just yet. My 5-year-old son, Michael, was having a serious asthma attack, and my wife, Mary, and I had to rush him to the hospital.

The doctors gave Michael a shot of adrenaline, but it took 15 or 20 minutes for it to take effect. It was not a pretty sight, watching your son fighting to get air into his lungs. Finally, his situation stabilized, he was able to breathe normally again, and we were able to take him home.

Michael had periodic asthma attacks until he was 13, but that was 35 years ago, and, thank God, he hasn't had an attack since.

By the time we pulled into our driveway, so thankful that he was breathing normally again, dawn was fast approaching. I fell into bed at 7:45, but my alarm went off 15 minutes later.

Thank goodness I wasn't playing that day.

Boy, was this sleepy ballplayer in for a rude awakening.

When I arrived at Dodger Stadium, there was my name in the starting lineup. Really? I found Alston and asked him what had happened to my day off.

"Wes Parker had an upset stomach and didn't have a good night's sleep," he said, "so I put you in the lineup."

I was thinking, *Wes* didn't have a good night's sleep? Hell, I haven't been to bed, barely put one wrinkle in my sheets. I had a headache from the celebration, took my son to the hospital, no sleep, no breakfast, nothing.

I didn't say any of that, because I knew it wasn't the fault of Walt or Wes. All I could do was put on my uniform, go out there and hope that, in what was basically an exhibition game, I wouldn't be required to do much.

What I didn't know was that Alston and Vin Scully had gotten together and decided that, because the game had no bearing on the standings, they would have some fun. Vinny not only would announce the game, but do some managing as well. They arranged a set of signs so that Vinny would let Alston know what he wanted to do in certain situations, and Alston would relay that on to the third-base coach.

All I wanted was for the game to be over so that I could go home, check on my son, and get some sleep. During batting practice, I made the Braves' starting pitcher, Bob Sadowski, an offer. Throw whatever you want and I'll swing at every pitch. I told him, I just want to get out of here.

When the game started, Vinny told the fans at the game who were listening on their transistor radios about the arrangement he had made with Alston. In the dugout, I could hear Vinny's voice, but I didn't pay much attention to what he was saying.

My first time up, I showed Sadowski that I was serious about what I had said. I swung at the first pitch. But he probably thought I had been trying to sucker him into easing off on me because the ball went into right field for a single.

In the third inning, I swung at a pitch low and outside, and blooped the ball into left field for a hit that drove in the first run of the game. I'm glad we had a lead, but I wasn't happy about the hit because I didn't feel well, and certainly didn't want to be on base.

With all the transistor radios blaring around me, I could hear Vinny's voice. He was talking about having me steal second base. Stealing a base was the last thing I wanted to do.

I looked at our third-base coach and, sure enough, I got the steal sign. With Lou Johnson at the plate, the pitcher went into his stretch, came set, started his delivery, and off I went, but the pitch was fouled back into the stands.

As I trotted back to first, I could hear Vinny again, "I'll bet the Braves don't expect Fairly to try to steal again," he was telling his audience. "Let's try it one more time."

Oh no, I got the steal sign again. Sadowski started his delivery and off I went again, and that pitch was also fouled away.

The fans and Vinny were having fun, and I would have had fun, too, with a couple of hours of sleep. But I was miserable. I hollered at Lou, "You're a better hitter that that. Hit the damn ball."

When I got back to first, I could hear Vinny laughing and saying, "Let's send Ron one more time." I looked at the third-base coach, and he gave me the steal sign. I shook my head no and gave him the safe sign, meaning I'm calling it off. I'm not going.

Vinny and the crowd got a good laugh out of that.

And so did I, when the game was mercifully over. We won, 3-0, and despite my determination to get every at-bat over quickly so I could get back to the dugout and close my eyes for a minute, I went 2-for-3.

Maybe I had discovered the secret to being a successful hitter: Get less sleep.

We opened the 1965 World Series against the Twins in Minnesota. If he had his choice, Alston would have started Koufax in Game 1, but Sandy would not pitch because the game fell on Yom Kippur, the holiest day of the year on the Jewish calendar. I think he made the correct decision by being true to his faith.

So Drysdale started. I didn't think it made that much of a difference. Sandy won 26 games that season, and Don won 23. Koufax/Drysdale or Drysdale/Koufax. Either way, they were going to pitch the first two games of the series. It was not an issue for the players.

The Twins started Jim "Mudcat" Grant, a 21-game winner. I homered in the second inning to give us a 1-0 lead, but that didn't last long. Minnesota tied it in the bottom of the second, then rolled out six runs in the third to knock Drysdale out of the game. When Alston came to the mound to make the pitching change, Don told him, "Right about now, I'll bet you're wishing I was Jewish."

The Twins went on to win, 8-2 .

Game 2 wasn't much better. Minnesota banged out nine hits and won, 5-1. Koufax was the losing pitcher even though he gave up only one earned run in six innings of work. Nevertheless, the Twins had beaten our two best pitchers. We were in trouble.

The turning point of the series didn't come on the field. It came at 30,000 feet.

On our flight back to Los Angeles for Games 3, 4, and 5, Gil Hodges, then the manager of the Washington Senators, was on our plane. Hodges, Drysdale's old Dodger roommate, wanted to see the scouting report on how we were pitching Twins hitters.

After reading it, he shook his head and said, "This is not a good report. You're pitching to the strength of some of these guys."

Because Gil was an American League manager, we were confident he knew what he was talking about. We were pitching some of their hitters backward. For example: Left fielder Sandy Valdespino was a left-handed hitter. The report said to pitch him inside because couldn't pull a good fastball.

Wrong.

In Game 1, Drysdale threw a fastball in on his hands, just as the report advised, and Valdespino pulled a hard line drive into the right-field corner. Unfortunately, I was playing him in right center because of the report. I had to run the ball down just to hold him to a double.

Center fielder Jimmie Hall, according to the report, has trouble hitting low fastballs, so that was what we threw him a majority of the time. "Jimmie," said Gil, "is one of the best low-fastball hitters in the American League."

The scouting report was wrong again.

Finally, here's the one that really made us scratch our heads.

According to the report, left fielder Bob Allison liked to wear his pants high around his knees, showing his stockings, and, therefore, he prefers the ball up in the strike zone.

*What?* What does how you wear your pants have to do with where you like pitches to hit? Gil said, "Allison is a good fastball hitter up or down. You have a better chance of getting him out with off-speed stuff or breaking balls."

Gil went through the entire report, making more suggestions.

We didn't want to make any excuses for losing the first two games or criticize anyone in the Dodger organization who had anything to do with the scouting report. So, we kept Gil's opinions quiet, limiting the information to our players. We certainly didn't want to see it in the media.

Before Game 3 at Dodger Stadium, we held a meeting to revise the entire scouting report.

For Claude Osteen, our starter that day, the whole thing was irrelevant. "I didn't even look at the scouting report," he said, "because I faced those guys when I was in the American League with the Senators and never lost to them."

Claude had been 5-0 against Minnesota in his four seasons with the Senators, and he kept his streak alive in Game 3, pitching a complete-game shutout as we won 4-0.

Games 4 and 5 were rematches of the first two games. It was again Drysdale against Grant in Game 4, and this time, Don got a complete-game victory, striking out 11 and winning 7-2. In Game 5, Koufax again matched up against Jim Kaat, and Sandy also got revenge. He started fast, retiring the first 12 batters and 18 of the first 19. Sandy went on to pitch a complete-game shutout, allowing four hits and striking out 10 as we won 7-0.

Back in Minnesota, we had a chance to wrap up the series in Game 6, especially with Grant coming back on just two days rest for his third start of the series. But he certainly didn't look like a tired pitcher. Not only did Mudcat pitch a complete game in a 5-1 Twins victory, but he supplied the coup de grâce by smacking a three-run homer.

It was decision time for Alston. Who should he start in Game 7, Drysdale on three days rest or Koufax with only two days rest?

Alston decided to start Sandy. The number of days of rest had nothing to do with it. Sandy was more muscular than Don, so it took him longer to warm up. This way, Alston figured, Sandy could take his time warming up at the start of the game and Don would be in the bullpen. If Sandy got into trouble, Don could get ready much faster.

Early in the game, Koufax struggled with his control and couldn't get his curveball over. Alston had Drysdale ready to come in a couple of times, but Sandy kept pitching out of jams, the Twins leaving five men on base in the first five innings. Throughout Koufax's career, if he was going to have trouble, it was generally in the early innings. This game was no different. After each inning, Alston asked Sandy how he felt and Sandy kept saying he was OK.

In the top of the fourth inning, "Sweet" Lou Johnson hit his second home run of the series to give us a 1-0 lead. I followed with a double to right, and Wes Parker followed with a single to right, enabling me to score.

Around the sixth inning, with Koufax still having trouble getting his curve over, he and Roseboro decided to just go with the fastball. From that point on, Roseboro didn't call for a single curve.

In the seventh, I was standing near the bat rack and heard Sandy tell Roseboro to keep calling fastballs. "I'm starting to hit spots, it's getting dark, and they haven't turned the lights on yet."

It turned out to be another typical Koufax performance with early struggles, but increased velocity in the final three or four innings. How strong was he toward the end? Sandy retired 14 of the last 15 batters he faced, getting a complete-game victory with 10 strikeouts.

Sandy may not have started the first game of the World Series, but he started and finished the last, giving us another world championship.

It was a different game when Koufax pitched. To beat him, the opposing team didn't have nine innings to score. They had only five or six. If they didn't get to him by then, they weren't going to.

I would love to have seen him pitching today. Would any manager dare to take him out in the sixth inning as they do most starters, knowing what Sandy probably still had in his tank?

He was a perfectionist, not only on the mound, but even with a razor in his hand. For example, when he shaved, his sideburns had to be just right.

Once during the year, I roomed with him. I was dressed and waiting for him to finish shaving so we could go out to eat. There was one contrary hair that he couldn't remove.

"Sandy," I said, "let's go. It's just one hair. My stomach is growling."

"It will just be a second," he said. Except it was more than that. It didn't matter. We couldn't go to dinner until he got that one hair.

Now let me tell you what kind of teammate he was.

In 1966, the Dodgers recalled a player named Jimmy Barbieri. Standing just 5 feet 7inches, and weighing 155 pounds, Jimmy played in 39 games for us and did a good job.

It was September and the Dodgers, Giants, and Pirates were in an extremely tight pennant race. Every game could mean the difference between getting to the World Series or staying home.

The pressure of the race was getting to Jimmy. One player heard him talking to himself in the shower after a close game, saying, "Why am I here? These guys are really good. I hope I don't screw up and lose the pennant for them."

A few days later, we were starting a three-game series against the Cardinals in St. Louis. Before batting practice, I was sitting in our dugout next to Sandy while some of the guys were stretching and getting their arms loose.

Sandy pointed at Barbieri and said, "I have a responsibility to him."

"Why?" I asked.

"If I pitch well between now and the end of the season," Sandy replied, "I can double his salary." He was talking about the World Series share Jimmy would receive if we got that far.

That September, Koufax was 6-1 with one no-decision, his only loss by a score of 2-1. He allowed an average of just 1.4 earned runs over the eight games.

We won the pennant by a game and a half, and Jimmy, who hit .280 for us, received his World Series share. It was a little extra special for him because he never returned to the majors after that season.

Sandy never told Jimmy that he was thinking about him. That would have been out of character for a man who never sought accolades. What it told me was that one of the biggest superstars the game has ever seen was just as concerned about the 25th man on the roster as he was about himself.

We struggled at the end of the regular season, winning only half of our final 16 games. It came down to the Dodgers and the Giants again on the final day.

We were in Philadelphia where we needed just one win in a double-header against the Phillies that day to punch our ticket to the World Series against the Baltimore Orioles. Drysdale started the first game, which we lost, 4-3, reliever Phil Regan giving up the game-clinching

RBI single in the eighth. As a result, Koufax was forced to pitch the nightcap — a win would eliminate San Francisco.

Meanwhile, the Giants, having beaten the Pirates for their sixth straight win, were sitting in a Pittsburgh airport, hoping their season wouldn't end there.

It was up to Sandy, as it so often was. He was again equal to the task, winning, 6-3, with 10 strikeouts to clinch the pennant. It was his 27th victory of the season, and his 27th complete game. For the Giants, there was nothing to do but get on their plane and go home.

The World Series started back home at Dodger Stadium three days later. Don pitched Game 1 and lost, 5-2.

Sandy pitched Game 2 and lost, 6-0. The most memorable, or rather forgettable, inning of that game was the fifth, when three errors by Willie Davis in center led to three runs. Two of the errors occurred when he lost fly balls in the sun. The last one was a bad throw to third, allowing a run to score. There were more errors in that inning (three) than hits (two).

In all, we committed six errors and failed to score a run, a thoroughly embarrassing performance on a national stage.

If we thought a change of scenery might change our spirits, we quickly learned that would not be the case.

Emphasis on quickly.

Game 3, played at Memorial Stadium in Baltimore, took only 1 hour and 55 minutes. We were shut out by a right-hander named Wally Bunker, 1-0, extending our scoreless streak in the series to 24 innings. The Orioles' only run came on a homer by Paul Blair.

Game 4 was much the same. Again, we were shut out, this time by left-hander Dave McNally. Again, the score was 1-0. Again, Baltimore got its only run on a homer, this time by Frank Robinson. Again, we went quickly and quietly, the game taking even less time than the last one, lasting just 1 hour and 45 minutes.

The way we hit that day, we could have used just one ball to play the entire game. It was typical of the whole series. We didn't score a single run after the third inning of Game 1, piling up 33 consecutive scoreless innings.

The Orioles became the 1966 World Series champions by sweeping us, and they earned it. They kicked our asses. They had a damn good team with players like Frank Robinson, Brooks Robinson, Boog Powell, Paul Blair, Davey Johnson, Luis Aparicio, and a solid pitching staff.

But wow, did we stink. I think that was the worst stretch of games I ever played in while wearing a Dodger uniform. I've never been on a team that was that inept. There were a lot of teams that could have beaten us in that World Series.

It hurt, but there would be other seasons. What really hurt was that we soon learned that there would be no other seasons for us with Sandy Koufax.

He decided that he was not going to continue pitching with a chronic elbow problem that required constant treatment and shots and pills, and could perhaps leave him without the use of that golden arm turned blue for the rest of his life.

He announced his retirement at the age of 30, and who could blame him.

# 11

## The Dodgers Brain Trust:
## Two Walters and a Buzzie

WALTER WAS WALTER O'MALLEY, Walt was Walt Alston, and Buzzie was Buzzie Bavasi. They had nothing in common in terms of background, temperament, or expertise. Yet working as a team, they created and maintained a dynasty that stretched from Brooklyn to Los Angeles. Each had his field of knowledge, each was brilliant in his own domain, and each respected the others' territory. Without all three, two of the most successful decades in Dodger history would probably never have occurred.

As a player, I took comfort in knowing they were my leaders. I knew that, if I did my job, I could remain part of an organization that would provide the profit margin, personnel and discipline to be successful.

### WALTER O'MALLEY

Mr. O'Malley was more than just a great owner for his own team. He was great for his sport as well, a transcendent figure who had the vision and the courage to make major league baseball a truly national sport by blazing the trail west when he moved the Dodgers to L.A., and persuaded Giants owner Horace Stoneham to join him by taking his team to San Francisco.

Mr. O'Malley had wanted to stay in Brooklyn and build a new, bigger stadium there to replace small, antiquated Ebbets Field. He was even considering building a domed stadium.

Robert Moses, the public official known as New York City's master builder, refused to approve Mr. O'Malley's plan. Moses wanted the new stadium to be built in the borough of Queens in the area where Shea Stadium was eventually constructed.

After all, Moses figured, what was Mr. O'Malley's realistic alternative?

Only the most groundbreaking decision in sports history, opening up the western half of the country from Seattle to San Diego to major league baseball with the NBA and NHL eventually to follow.

I had a great relationship with Mr. O'Malley.

In the early 1960s, he got hooked on playing golf and built a nine-hole course in Vero Beach. Later, he built the 18-hole course we all played on down the street from the Dodgertown complex.

There was only one stipulation for the players. No golf carts for us. We had to walk. The front-office people felt the extra walking would strengthen our legs. No argument about that.

On the day of Mr. O'Malley's annual golf tournament and barbecue at Dodgertown, Alston limited our baseball activities to a short workout so that those of us who wanted to head to the golf course would be free to do so.

It was only supposed to be a half-day of work for the players. Not for me. That morning, the coaches worked my ass off. They had me shagging extra fly balls and fielding extra ground balls They never hit balls to me, instead hitting them to my left and to my right so I had to run after them. Instead of running 10 wind sprints, I had to do 15.

When I was done, I took a quick shower and rushed to the golf course just in time to tee off. I found out I was playing with Mr. O'Malley, team Vice President Jim Mulvey, and Monsignor John Patrick Kelly. The stakes were $5 a man.

"How was your workout today?" Mr. O'Malley asked when I arrived at the tee box. "I told the coaches to run you a little more so you would be tired."

Obviously, he was not my partner.

On the first hole, I hit a good drive that landed in the fairway. I started walking to my ball while everyone else was riding in their carts. Remember, as a player, I wasn't allowed to use a cart.

When I reached my ball, I saw it was embedded in the ground. Mr. O'Malley had driven his cart over it. "We are playing summer rules," he told me as I reached into my bag for a club. "That means play the ball as it lies."

As he took off, he laughed over his shoulder and told me I could move my ball.

We had a good time, and, yes, Mr. O'Malley won the money.

At the barbecue that night, Monsignor Kelly told me about his experiences playing golf with Mr. O'Malley.

"He sends the Dodger plane to New York to pick me up," the monsignor said, "brings me here for a couple of weeks, pays for my food and lodging, entertains me, and then takes my money on the golf course. He's always in charge of keeping everyone's score and there were a couple of rounds where I think it may have been Mr. O'Malley's pencil that beat me.

"I've kept some of the scorecards and, one of these days, he will come to confession and I'm going to talk to him about my scores."

It was all in fun, but Mr. O'Malley liked to compete and didn't like to lose. That was evident from the way he ran his ballclub.

I had so much respect for Monsignor Kelly that I named one of my sons, Patrick, after him.

Every spring, the minor league players were taken to Holman Stadium for a lecture about the rules of the camp, what time to eat, and how to protect their valuables. They were told that they should take their money or jewelry to the Dodger offices. The ladies there would put their valuable items in an envelope and put it in the safe.

One day at lunch time, a young minor league player took his money to the office, but it was closed. As the player stood there, trying to decide what to do, in walked Walter O'Malley.

"Can I help you, young man?" he asked.

"I'm waiting for the office to open so I can put my cash in the safe," the player said.

"Give it to me," said Mr. O'Malley with a big smile on his face, "and I'll put your money in the safe."

The player, looking at this man who was wearing khaki pants and a flowered shirt, was out of shape, and didn't appear to belong in a baseball training camp, said, "Not on your life, fatso. I've just been told to watch out for guys like you."

The player left, only to be told later whom he had been talking to. After that, every time Mr. O'Malley came into the lobby when players were congregating, the young player got up and left, fearful of a confrontation.

Finally, Mr. O'Malley called him into his office and told him that he had done the right thing by hanging onto his money. Mr. O'Malley said that if he should walk into the lobby when the player was there, he wanted the player to please stay there and relax.

When we beat the Yankees four straight in the 1963 World Series at Dodger Stadium, the victory party was held that evening at the Stadium Club.

I had a decent year, hitting .271 with 12 home runs and 77 RBIs in 152 games. But that wasn't going to stop Mr. O'Malley from having a little fun with me.

While Fresco Thompson, our director of minor league operations, was addressing the crowd, I was standing next to Mr. O'Malley. He leaned over and said, "Ron, when Fresco finishes, I want you to speak on behalf of the players who probably won't be here next year."

"Thanks," I told him, "we just won the World Series 2½ hours ago, and you're already trying to get rid of me."

## WALT ALSTON

When Alston was hired to manage the Dodgers before the 1954 season, the headline in a New York newspaper was, "Alston (Who's He?) New Dodger Manager."

New York's lack of familiarity with Alston was understandable, considering that he had only one at-bat in the majors (he struck out), and had never even coached at the big league level. But he had been a minor

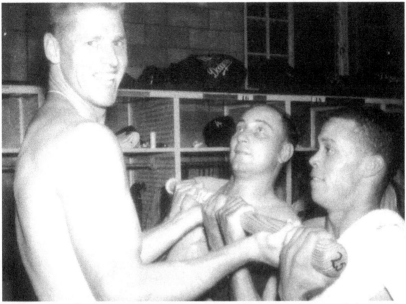

In 1962, Dodgers Frank Howard, left, Johnny Podres, and Maury Wills, right, test their strength with Manager Walt Alston's bat challenge.

league manager for 13 seasons.

The skepticism over Alston's hiring turned to doubt when, after taking over the two-time defending National League champions, he finished second in his first season to the New York Giants, who won 97 games, then swept the Cleveland Indians in the World Series.

But, with a quiet confidence, Alston shut up his critics by leading his team to the 1955 National League pennant. He then did something no other Dodger manager had ever done — he won a world championship for Brooklyn, and did it by beating the hated Yankees.

In all, Alston, in his 23 years as Dodger manager, won seven pennants and four world championships.

Someone meeting Walt for the first time would undoubtedly see a mild-mannered, soft-spoken man. But those of us who traveled with him and worked under his supervision knew that beneath the calm surface lay emotional strength and unwavering determination.

Those assets are a prerequisite for successfully managing a major league team.

Walt also possessed impressive physical strength, perhaps a byproduct of working as a young man on his family's Ohio farm.

Some of us on the Dodgers felt that strength literally firsthand when we accepted his challenge to test ourselves against him in a contest involving a bat.

Here's how it worked: Walt and a player stood about 4 feet apart with a bat between them that was parallel to the ground and held firmly with both hands by both men above their heads. The bat was then lowered to waist level.

When that happens, the bat will twist or spin in the hands of the weaker grip.

Walt never lost, never had the weaker grip. Not once.

One day, I challenged the skipper, but I cheated. I put pine tar on my hands so that the bat wouldn't spin in my grip. It worked ... for a few seconds. The bat didn't spin, but, because of Walt's powerful grip, my wrists rolled under the bat, and I went to my knees.

I lost, truly impressed at how strong he was.

When I said Walt Alston was a mild-mannered man, I should have clarified that by saying, until he was pissed.

In 1963, we lost a doubleheader to the Pirates on a hot, humid day in Pittsburgh. Driving to the airport on our way out of town, we were in an older bus that was slow and had a broken air-conditioning unit. The situation reminded me of that horrendous bus ride I was on from Albuquerque to Des Moines as a member of the Bruins, my first minor league team.

We were about a third of the way to the airport when the Pirates zoomed past us in a new Greyhound bus. Our players started making snide comments directed at Lee Scott, our traveling secretary. That lasted about 10 minutes.

Walt told the bus driver to pull over to the side of the highway and stop. As far as Walt was concerned, a team that loses a doubleheader has no business griping about the transportation out of town.

He stood up and challenged the entire team. "If anybody doesn't like this bus or anything else about how this team is managed," he said, "please step outside and we'll settle the issue here on the highway."

He went outside, stood out there for about seven or eight minutes, smoking a cigarette and waiting.

Nobody got off the bus. We just sat there sweating in the heat.

Walt finally got back on the bus. The rest of the trip to the airport and the flight back to Los Angeles were quiet and uneventful.

At spring training every year, Walt held a meeting to remind all the players how he expected them to act on the field. The meeting didn't last long because he only had a few basic points to get across.

He let the players know he would be very upset if they missed signs. He made them simple and easy to pick up so that nobody could plead ignorance about what they were supposed to do. And he demonstrated each one.

In his 23 years managing the Dodgers, Walt never changed his sign for the squeeze play. When he wanted to put that play on, he put both hands over his face.

He used that for two reasons. One, because it would be nearly impossible for the third-base coach to miss seeing that sign, and two, because we screwed it up so many times, Walt didn't want to see what happened.

The third-base coach would signal the batter that the squeeze was on. The runner at third would be alerted orally when the third-base coach walked over and called him by his last name only.

The play was normally designed with a fast runner like Maury Wills or Willie Davis on third. The 6-foot-7-inch, 255-pound Frank Howard was certainly not in that category. So, when he reached third, the last thing he was thinking about was taking off for the plate on a bunt.

Who would ever think the Dodgers would put on a squeeze play with Big Frank on third? Exactly the reason Alston decided to try it.

Pete Reiser, our third-base coach, said, "Be alive, Howard, there's one out."

Said Frank, "Hey, Pete, you've known me long enough to call me by my first name."

Reiser, unable to contain himself, started laughing.

Frank looked at Reiser mystified until the third-base coach leaned over and whispered into Frank's ear that the squeeze was on.

After all that, it actually worked. Frank scored on the play.

Good thing he did because he would not have wanted to face Alston if he had blown it.

Nothing angered Alston as much as players who didn't hustle. He told us that this game is not that difficult. "Some of you will hit home runs," he'd say, "and if you want to take your time jogging around the bases, then take your time. However, if you hit a ball in fair territory, I WANT YOU TO RUN, AND RUN HARD." It doesn't take talent to run a play out.

There was a period when Walt didn't talk to me much. A couple of times, he walked past me and didn't even say hello or good morning. So one day, I asked him if he was mad at me, if I had done something that upset him.

"No, I'm very pleased with the way you've been playing," he said. "As a manager, I don't have to spend a lot of time with those who play every day. I don't have to say anything to guys like you. The fact that I put your name in the starting lineup says that I have confidence in you to play well and help us. I have to spend more time with the guys who are not in the lineup to keep them ready for when I do need them."

That one conversation taught me a lot about managing.

Walt's basic philosophy, as I heard him express it to the baseball writers, was, "If I don't get in their way, these guys know how to play and will win a lot of games. My job is keep them focused."

I think one of his strengths was his willingness to say nothing. I mean that as a compliment. I know we did things from time to time that really aggravated him. But when the game was over, he never said anything to a player who had let him down. He waited until the next day and, if it still bothered him, he talked to the player, figuring that, a day removed from the game, he might be more receptive to what Walt had to say. Most of the time, he allowed the little things to slip by as long as we were winning games. We had leaders on the team who took care of the small stuff, guys like Pee Wee, Duke, Gil, Sandy, Don, Maury, John Roseboro, and Jim Gilliam. Each had his own way of talking to other players.

Walt not only knew when to not say anything to a player he was upset with, he also knew how to get his message across by not doing anything.

On a trip to Chicago to play the Cubs, the Dodger manager got a call at 2 a.m. from the local police department. He was informed that one

**Third baseman Andy Carey was with the Dodgers for only one season, 1962, and his photos that year captured the team's post-victory clubhouse high jinks.**

of his pitchers was behind bars after being arrested for being drunk in public. Did the manager want to come and bail out the player?

"No," Walt told the police official, "I'll come by in the morning to get him on my way to the ballpark."

I don't remember Alston ever calling a team meeting when we were on a winning streak. So when he did call us together, we knew what we were about to hear wouldn't be politically correct. If somebody got his feelings hurt, Walt didn't care. He had to get things off his chest, and didn't give a shit what we thought.

When the meeting started, he would light a cigarette. If his hands were shaking when he flicked the match, we knew we were in trouble. He would look around the room at all of us, point out things that we screwed up as far back as two or three weeks earlier, and let us know what he felt about that.

Walt would never criticize anybody's ability. It was always about effort, about not hustling, about missing signs, about throwing to the wrong base, about drinking and staying out late.

When the meeting was over, Drysdale and I would try to figure out who Walt was talking about the most.

After one meeting, Don asked, "How many of the things the skipper mentioned applied to you?"

I said, "He got me for two of them."

Replied Don, "He got me for three."

The most difficult team meeting I ever attended came after we lost a few games in the midst of a tight pennant race by making some bone-head plays. We looked like the 1962 Mets.

As Walt lit his cigarette, our clubhouse man, John "The Senator" Griffin, positioned himself behind the manager.

It was a typical lecture by Walt, talking about our lack of concentration and hustle, and our disregard of curfew. As the manager gave us hell, The Senator started to make faces at him.

It was difficult not to snicker, to continue looking serious and contrite. When Walt glanced back at The Senator, the clubhouse man had a give-it-to-them, they-deserve-it look on his face. But as soon as Walt looked back at us, The Senator gave him the finger. Most players kept their heads down, staring at the floor, because they couldn't look at Walt without seeing The Senator. And they knew, if they looked at The Senator, they would burst into laughter. No telling how Walt would have reacted to that, but it wouldn't have been good.

The meeting lasted about 30 minutes. When it was over, several players, having been distracted by The Senator, couldn't remember what Walt had said.

"I think," said one player, "it was something about really playing horse shit and, if we don't play better, we're not going to the World Series."

Somehow, the message got through because we won 15 of our next 20 games.

Of all the managers I had, Walt was the easiest to play for. All he wanted you to do was show up ready to play and keep your mind in the game. I really enjoyed my years with him. He gave me every opportunity to succeed. That's all I could ask for. The rest was up to me.

## BUZZIE BAVASI

He was given the name Emil Joseph at birth, but was nicknamed Buzzie by his sister, Iola, because she said he was always buzzing around. He lived up to the name, buzzing around baseball for 41 years.

A native New Yorker, he began his career as an office boy with the Brooklyn Dodgers, then became an executive in the team's minor league system before heading off to military service, where he won a bronze star as a machine-gunner in World War II.

When Buzzie returned, he became general manager of the Nashua Dodgers, a Class B farm team in New Hampshire playing in the New England League. It was there that he caught the attention of Branch Rickey when he agreed to put Roy Campanella and Don Newcombe on his roster after a Dodgers farm team in Danville, Illinois, refused to accept them because they were black.

If they can play better than what we have here, Bavasi reportedly said, we don't care what color they are.

In his 18 years as the Brooklyn/Los Angeles Dodgers GM, the team won eight pennants and four world championships.

On the day of a night game at Dodger Stadium, Johnny Podres, Al Ferrara, and a couple of other players went to Hollywood Park racetrack.

They didn't know that Buzzie was also there, up in a suite. He knew they were there because he could look down and see them.

As the fifth race was coming up, Buzzie realized it was time to leave. He always liked to get to the stadium early, and with weekday rush hour on L.A. freeways fast approaching, traffic delays were inevitable. So, he left before the race began and still arrived at Dodger Stadium 45 minutes later than he normally did. He knew that the four players he had observed would be even later, because his last sight of them was in line at the betting window for the fifth race.

Buzzie went down to the clubhouse and left notes in the lockers of each of the four players. Each note read, "When you get to the ballpark, don't get dressed. Come to my office."

If you're a ballplayer, that's not a note you ever want to see.

When the players walked into the office, Buzzie acted as if he was mad.

"Why were you guys late?" he asked. "You could be looking at a $100 fine."

"We went to the track," Johnny said.

"OK, when did you leave?" he asked

All four claimed to have left early enough to get to the stadium on time.

"Then why did you get here late?" asked Buzzie.

"Uh, we had a flat tire," said Johnny.

Buzzie tore a sheet of paper into four pieces, handed one to each of the players along with a pen, sent them to different corners of the room, and said, "Write down which tire was flat."

They each wrote down a different tire.

Buzzie informed them that they'd each be looking at a $100 fine if the Dodgers lost that night.

They won.

Over the years, when Johnny had a hot tip on a horse and needed a little cash, he borrowed money from Buzzie.

In 1980, Buzzie and I were both with the Angels, he as the general manager and I as an announcer. I was in Buzzie's office killing time before the game when Podres called him from the East Coast.

"I'm at Belmont Park," Johnny said, "and my jockey friend told me about a horse running tomorrow that is primed and should win. The odds are good, too. I know I owe you $500. What do you want me to do?"

"Are you sure the tip is good?" Buzzie asked him.

"Yes," said Johnny.

"Then go ahead and bet the 500 bucks," said Buzzie.

When he hung up, Buzzie looked at me and said, "I just lost 500 bucks."

"How do you know?" I asked him. "The race isn't until tomorrow."

"Because," said Buzzie, "Johnny never told me the name of the horse."

When Al Campanis was the Dodgers' scouting director, he had photographs lining the walls of his office of all the players he discovered or signed who went on to successful careers.

When Campanis went on a winter vacation one year, Buzzie came into his office looking for something and saw all those photographs.

As soon as someone in the front office reached a point of feeling a little too good about themselves, a little too cocky, Buzzie had a way of taking them down a notch or two.

So, he went into the Dodgers' photo files and pulled out pictures of some of the players Campanis had signed who turned out to be busts. Buzzie replaced Campanis' photos with this batch of disappointing players.

Fresco Thompson was another member of the Dodgers brain trust for many years. A second baseman in the majors for the Dodgers and several other teams in the 1920s and '30s, he worked his way up in the Dodger organization after his playing days were over, learning under Branch Rickey.

The owner of a local men's store attending a spring training game in Vero Beach was in his box seat when a foul ball rolled toward him. He leaned over, trying to field the ball, but couldn't get a firm grasp on it. It rolled a couple of feet away, reaching the edge of the field. The merchant stepped out of his box onto the field, picked up the ball, and returned to his seat. Fresco watched the entire incident, but said nothing.

The next day, Fresco walked into the man's store, looked around, spotted a shirt he liked on a shelf, picked it up, and started to walk out the door.

"Excuse me, Mr. Thompson," said the owner, "but didn't you forget something?"

"No," insisted Fresco, shaking his head, "Yesterday, you came into my place of business and took my merchandise, and today, I'm doing the same thing to you."

Fresco gave the shirt to one of the cooks in the Dodgertown kitchen.

# *12*

## New Uniforms,
## New Challenges

A THOUGH BOTH MR. O'MALLEY and Buzzie often enjoyed a good laugh with other members of the organization and were never shy about needling them or pulling a prank, there were limits to their patience when rules or requests were ignored.

Sometimes the punishment was a fine. But in the case of Maury Wills, it was much more severe.

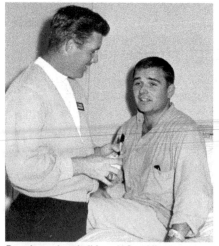

Ron signs a baseball for a U.S. soldier hospitalized in Japan during a Dodgers goodwill tour in 1966.

Our 1966 collapse in the World Series was followed by a goodwill trip to Japan. We didn't play much better over there.

We weren't there to win a pennant or even dominate the opposition. But Mr. O'Malley didn't want to be embarrassed by our play, either. We wound up barely above .500 on that trip, finishing 9-8-1. And remember, this was before the level of play in Japan had significantly improved, making that nation's baseball program competitive on the world stage.

We were not at full strength in Japan. Koufax was back in L.A. preparing to retire, and Drysdale, Don Sutton, and Wes Parker had also stayed home.

Maury was on the trip, but a knee injury he had suffered during the season flared up. After appearing in only four of the games, he wanted to go back home to be examined, but Mr. O'Malley asked him to remain with the team.

"I would appreciate it very much," Mr. O'Malley told him, "if you would stay and be introduced before each game so that the Japanese fans can see you. You don't have to play and you can see the doctor when the team gets home."

Maury decided he was going to leave despite Mr. O'Malley's appeal.

At the time, Buzzie and his wife, Evit, were going to Hawaii on vacation. When they got there, Buzzie heard that Maury was also there, playing his banjo in a bar in the Hawaiian Village.

Buzzie informed Mr. O'Malley that, rather than being in L.A. getting his knee examined, Maury was in Hawaii performing.

He may have been a record-breaking star who had been on three world champion Dodger teams, but he had crossed the line as far as Dodger management was concerned.

"A higher degree of devotion to duty was expected," said Mr. O'Malley of Maury, then the team's captain.

Shortly after the team returned home from Japan, Maury was traded to the Pirates for Bob Bailey and Gene Michael.

## MONTREAL EXPOS

At 2 p.m. on a June afternoon in 1969, my life changed. I received a phone call from the Dodgers telling me that I had been traded to the Montreal Expos. What a horrible, dark day that was in my life.

It was a bright day, though, in the life of Maury Wills. I had been traded, along with Paul Popovich for Maury and Manny Mota. After 2½ years in exile, Maury had been forgiven and was coming home.

When Mr. O'Malley died in 1979, Maury paid tribute to him, and said that the Dodger owner had taught him a valuable lesson in life by shipping him out of town.

"He built a golf course at Vero Beach," said Maury of Mr. O'Malley, "so black players, who couldn't play on local courses, could play there. Blacks and whites always roomed together on the Dodgers when other clubs weren't yet doing this. On the Dodger plane, you got fed, but still got your meal money. Other clubs would deduct the plane food from your meal allowance. In spring training, Mr. O'Malley would have your clothes cleaned and still give you a cleaning allowance.

"I never felt vindictive [about the trade]. He was the boss and, even though he was kind and generous, he taught me you just don't cross him."

It felt terrible driving to Dodger Stadium, going into the clubhouse, packing my equipment, and saying goodbye to my teammates after being there for 10½ years. It was not easy to say farewell to so many familiar faces, so I packed as fast as I could.

After more than 10 years with the Dodgers, in 1969 Ron was traded to the Montreal Expos. The team played in a foreign city where he didn't speak the primary language, and where the climate was foreign to a Southern Californian.

For my entire life, I had been associated with winning teams — in little league, high school, college, professionally — with very few exceptions. Now I was leaving a team that had a chance to win 100 games to go to an expansion team that was expected to lose 100 games. How does one mentally handle losing that many games? I was also being traded out of the country to an area where the primary language was French, a language I didn't speak.

Ron Fairly and Tom Seaver, right, both played for USC, but not on the same team. They did play together at the 1973 All-Star Game in Kansas City, Fairly as an Expo, Seaver as a Met.

Yet none of that was as bad as what happened that night at home as I was packing to join the Expos. I was showing my boys where I would be playing on a map of North America. I pointed to where we lived on the West Coast, and to where I was going to play in Montreal. My middle son, Mike, 6 at the time, looked up at me and said, "Does this mean I don't have a daddy anymore?"

That really hurt. It took a long time to get that out of my head.

Everyone has a little fear about going into the unknown. I knew nothing about Montreal, and had never met 80 percent of the players, but, at least I knew the manager, Gene Mauch.

The team played at a temporary facility called Jarry Park, a stadium not up to major league standards. It was a single-deck ballpark that seated just over 29,000.

It was a big adjustment just to get used to the weather. In subsequent seasons with the Expos, some home night games early in the season were played in temperatures in the 30s and low 40s. It was difficult to get loose, and if I didn't hit the ball on the sweet spot, the bat would hurt my hands. I ordered bats with skinnier handles and wore ski gloves to hit. It took a couple of seasons to realize how important a base on balls was early in the season.

On June 28, only a week before the Fourth of July, I came out of a restaurant after a night game, and it was snowing. I said to myself, When does summer get here? Growing up in Southern California, I had never been in temperatures that consistently cold.

When I got back home, my friends asked me what kind of a summer I had in Montreal. I told them I had a great summer — I hit .667, four hits in six at-bats, but unfortunately, that summer lasted just two days.

I learned to handle the cold weather, but I never learned to handle the losing. Going hitless and winning was a lot more tolerable than getting a hit and losing.

Unfortunately, I learned that winning was not that important for some of my new teammates. They were more concerned about their average, a hooray-for-me-and-the-hell-with-you attitude. Playing for an expansion team was a lot different from playing for a team fighting for a pennant.

One spring in Vero Beach when I was with the Dodgers, Mr. O'Malley approached a group of players, myself included, said he wanted to do a card trick, and asked me if I had a $5 bill.

When I pulled one out, he said, "Look at the serial numbers on the bill and remember the last four numbers." Then, he asked me to fold the bill in half so he couldn't see the numbers. Turning away, he extended his hand behind him and asked me to put the bill in it. Then, still looking away, he carefully unraveled the five and said, "Is this the bill you gave me?"

I said it was.

"Thank you," said Mr. O'Malley. He then put it in his pocket and walked away, leaving me standing there, thinking, What just happened?

The next morning, when I came out of the clubhouse, there he was in his golf cart talking to a group of writers.

"Good morning, Ron," said Mr. O'Malley. Turning to the writers, he told them, "Last night, I showed Ron a trick and he gave me $5."

"Someday," I told him, "I'll get it back."

When the Dodgers came to Montreal for the first time after I had been traded, I learned that Lee Scott, the team's traveling secretary, was taking the L.A writers out to dinner at the Beaver Club in the Queen Elizabeth Hotel.

I made reservations for a half-hour earlier, and ordered dinner. When the bill came, I wrote a note on it, saying, "This is for trading me out of the country," then told the waiter to give the bill to the man with the mustache at the large table on the other side of the room. When Scottie got the bill, he looked around, saw me a few tables away, shook his head, laughed, and put the bill next to his plate.

Weeks later, we were playing the Dodgers in L.A. When I got to the ballpark, there was a message in my locker from Mr. O'Malley, asking me to call him as soon as I got to the park. I hadn't talked to him since I was traded.

When I called his office, he came on the line. He didn't even begin the conversation by saying hello. He just said, "I thought I got rid of you."

"You did," I replied.

"Then how come you're still on the expense account," he said.

"Lee Scott must have told you," I said. "Thanks, it was a great dinner and I got back the five bucks you took from me in Vero Beach a few years ago."

We both laughed, then Mr. O'Malley got serious. "Ron, I didn't like the trade with Montreal," he said, "but I hire people to do their job and I don't interfere. When the season is over, please come to my office and bring your boys. Good luck to you the rest of the season, but not against my Dodgers."

When the season ended, I took two of my boys, Mike and 10-year-old Steve, to meet Mr. O'Malley. When I got to Dodger Stadium, he made me wait in his outer office while he played with the boys in his office for about 15 minutes.

Then we spoke for a few minutes, and he ended our conversation by saying, "When you finish playing baseball, I'll have a job for you."

My playing career ended the year Mr. O'Malley passed away.

He was highly respected among the other owners, and a tough negotiator with the players union, but he was very fond of his players and their families. He treated me great and made me feel very proud to be part of the Dodger family.

I enjoyed playing for Gene Mauch in Montreal. When he came to the ballpark, he was ready to manage and he expected his players to be ready to play. Gene probably knew the rules of the game better than any manager I ever played for.

During games, he carefully watched the way players ran on and off the field. One day, I asked him why he did that. He said, "It tells me a lot about how the player feels about himself and the game." That was interesting, and for the rest of my career, I always watched the way players ran on and off the field.

Gene had a keen eye for every player. He was always evaluating our skills — does a pitcher throw as hard as he used to? Has a player lost a step or two running the bases? Do pull hitters still pull fastballs?

That's how he was evaluating me, I learned, during spring training of 1971. I was pretty much a pull hitter for my whole career, but that spring, I was working to hit the ball up the middle. After a few exhibition games, Gene said to me, "You're not pulling the ball as much."

"I'm not trying to pull the ball like I used to," I told him.

"Yeah," he said, "and you've never been 33 years old before. Show me you can still hit the fastball."

That pissed me off, so for the next couple of games I pulled every fastball as far foul as I could. I hit some 75 or 100 feet foul. After a while, Gene said, "OK, asshole, go ahead and hit the ball back up the middle."

I won that battle, but it made me realize what the war was really about. Gene was right to question why I was trying to do something different after all those years. He was wondering if my ability to pull fastballs might be diminishing, and that maybe it was time to trade me to another team.

Gene could be tough on a struggling player. One time, the Expos called up a young Latin prospect from the minor leagues to fill a vacancy on the roster. During batting practice before a game against the Giants in Candlestick Park, he had a difficult time hitting the ball far enough to reach the fence and was not in the starting lineup.

In the ninth inning, Gene sent this young player up to pinch hit for the pitcher. He swung late on the first pitch, was late again on the second, and the third pitch was in the catcher's mitt before he could even swing. Strike three. The player was obviously overmatched.

It turned out that the Expos had accidentally called up the wrong player which frustrated Gene even more.

After the game, he called the player into his office and asked, "Can you catch?"

The young man said, "Yes sir!"

"Good," said Gene, "I want you to catch the 7 o'clock flight back to the minor leagues."

He could be very tough on umpires as well.

In one game, our shortstop, Tim Foli, was called out sliding into second. From the dugout, he appeared to be safe. Gene charged out to dispute the call. He argued for a minute or two, but the ump was not going to change his mind.

When the umpire told Gene to get off the field, he replied, "Not before I ask you something. If I were to call you a bunch of dirty names right now, would you kick me out of the game?"

"Yes," said the umpire.

"If I were to think of a bunch of dirty names about you, would you kick me out of the game?"

"No."

"Well," said Gene, "I think you're a no-good, rotten %&#%@%$# SOB."

He was ejected from the game.

We had a stretch of games when we couldn't do anything right. If we scored some runs, we had no pitching. If we had good pitching, we didn't score any runs. If we had pitching and hitting, we had no defense. We finally had a game where we put it all together — we had no hitting, no pitching, and no defense.

Gene couldn't stand losing any longer, and I didn't blame him. When the game was over, he stormed into his office and slammed the door so hard that everyone could feel it. Three or four minutes later, he came out and stared at all of us for a few seconds. The clubhouse was silent. Nobody moved.

"For your information," Gene told us, "I've tried to trade everyone in this room and not one team wanted any one of you. We only have eight major league players in the room."

He turned around, went back into his office, and slammed the door again. Silence returned while everyone looked around to see who Gene might have been talking about.

My roommate, Gary Sutherland, came over to my locker and whispered, "What Gene just said is a damn lie."

"What at you talking about?" I asked.

Said Sutherland, "We don't have eight major league players in this room."

On a trip to Chicago, Gene, having heard of a popular nightspot where players were known to meet young ladies, decided to stop by one night after curfew.

Sure enough, there was one of his starting pitchers, deep in conversation with a couple of women.

Confronting the player, Gene said, "Are you having a good time?"

The player, knowing it was futile to deny it, said, "Yes."

"Are you having $100 worth of fun?" Gene asked him.

"No," said the player, who then turned to the ladies and said, apologetically, "I have to go."

"No, you don't," said Gene. "You've already been caught and fined. You might as well stay here all night if you like and get your money's worth."

Managers were always on the lookout for curfew violators. A familiar trick many of them used was to give an unmarked baseball to the elevator operator in the team hotel and tell that person to ask for autographs from all players who came in after curfew.

The next day, the manager would retrieve the ball, giving him a list of all those who missed curfew. The players couldn't argue. They had, in effect, signed a confession that they were guilty.

There were times in Montreal after a game when I just wanted to go somewhere quiet. Didn't want to be around anyone. Just wanted to be by myself.

One late afternoon following a day game, I went to one of the nicest hotels downtown to relax and have dinner. In the cocktail lounge,

I saw the visiting manager sitting at the far end of the bar with a lady. We made eye contact, but that was it. I sat at the opposite end of the bar and drank my cocktail.

A few minutes later, the manager paid his tab, and the couple started to leave. The lady walked past me, but the manager stopped to whisper in my ear, "Managers have dicks, too, you know."

After spending 5½ seasons in Montreal, I was traded to the St. Louis Cardinals in December of 1974 for infielder Rudy Kinard and first baseman/outfielder Ed Kurpiel, both minor leaguers.

The fans in Montreal were great. The first couple of years I was there, we had a parade downtown at the start of the season. The fans lined the streets and cheered as we drove by. In the years I played there, I met some very nice people. It was a shame we didn't play as well as the fans supported us.

## ST. LOUIS CARDINALS

After all my years with Drysdale, playing for the Cardinals gave me my first chance to see the other half of baseball's most intimidating pair of pitchers, Bob Gibson, up close and personal.

It didn't take long for me to be thankful I was on Gibson's side. With him as our starting pitcher in our very first game in spring training, in the very first inning, facing the very first batter, with the very first pitch, he lived up to his reputation.

Frank Taveras, leading off for the Pirates, tried to push a bunt past Gibson, toward the second baseman. Gibson responded with a fastball, inside, that hit Taveras in the chest near his heart. Down he went, and I said to myself, Oh my God, it took only one pitch for Gibson to hit somebody.

Taveras rolled around on the ground for a minute, got up, and went to first. It was the last time any Pirate tried to bunt on Gibson that day.

After the game, he said, "It's spring training. Tell him to swing the bat. He can practice bunting off someone else."

Gibson's approach was simple. He was a power pitcher, threw strikes, and didn't waste a lot of time between pitches. He worked fast and didn't like hitters to step out of the batter's box. If they dared to do so, he'd let them know he wasn't happy. Gibson's philosophy was: Here it is, see if you can hit it. Either I've got you or you've got me. Let's find out.

When he pitched, the games lasted two hours or less.

One afternoon in a game in which Tim McCarver was catching Gibson, the opposing team had a runner with speed at first with two outs. McCarver looked into his dugout and saw his manager, Johnny Keane, give the sign for a pitchout.

McCarver flashed that sign to Gibson, who responded by shaking his head no. McCarver flashed the pitchout sign again, and again, Gibson shook it off. McCarver pointed to the dugout, indicating the sign came from the manager, and for the third time, gave the pitchout sign.

From the mound, Gibson shouted at McCarver, "You won't throw him out anyway."

The catcher grudgingly nodded, gave the sign for a fastball, and Gibson got the batter out.

As of the 1975 season, Ron was a St. Louis Cardinal, and a teammate of the unpredictable and intimidating pitcher Bob Gibson.

That was Gibson. He didn't care about the runner at first. Get the hitter out, and the inning was over.

In my first game at first base for the Cardinals, with Gibson pitching, I was told to not go anywhere near the mound. It was his territory, and he didn't want to share it. And he certainly didn't want to hear from any of his teammates.

Midway through the game, I ended up near the mound at the end of a play. I decided to invade his space, despite the warning I had been given. "I'm not here to say anything," I told him. "I just need to put some rosin on my hands because they're sweaty."

I picked up the rosin bag while Gibson stood there, hands on his hips, staring at me.

"Got enough?" he said impatiently.

"Yes," I replied.

"Then," he said with a glare, "get off my mound!"

Another of my new teammates was Lou Brock. It was fascinating to watch him operate, to see how precise he was stealing bases.

Lou used a stopwatch to time opposing pitchers to see how long it took them to deliver the ball from a stretch position to the catcher. According to Lou, for most pitchers, it was 1.5 seconds. He timed the catchers to see how long it took them to throw the ball to second base. Most catchers were clocked at 2.0 seconds. So, from the time the ball left the pitcher's hand to the instant it was in the glove of the shortstop or second baseman, took 3.5 seconds.

Lou was able to run the 90 feet from first to second in 3.25 seconds on a consistent basis. So logically, even with a solid execution among pitcher, catcher, and infielder, he would be safe by .25 of a second. Perfect execution, a misstep by Lou, or a bad call by the umpire could result in an out. But pitchers who took more than 1.5 seconds to deliver the pitch gave their catchers no chance to nail him.

## OAKLAND ATHLETICS

After nearly two full seasons with the Cardinals, I was on the move again, sold to the Oakland Athletics for the final 2½ weeks of the 1976 season. After 18 years in the majors, I was playing in the American League for the first time.

I quickly learned how difficult it could be to get a good salary from owner Charlie Finley

"I was making only $27,000 a year, and I appeared in 70 games as his closer," reliever Rollie Fingers told me. "Later, I found out Finley paid $29,000 for that mule mascot he liked. He paid more for the mule than he did for me. That really pissed me off, and I vowed I'd never play for Finley again."

He didn't. At the end of that season, Fingers became a free agent, and signed with the Padres.

We had a youngster who worked for the team from 1971 to 1980. He started out as a batboy when he was 9. It was a dream job for him, as it would be for most kids. But this young man also had other dreams, bigger dreams.

The kid, a local young man named Stanley Burrell, was nicknamed Little Hammer by the players because of his facial resemblance to Hammerin' Hank Aaron.

It was Finley who first discovered Burrell dancing in the stadium parking lot, invited him inside, and eventually he became executive vice president. Burrell stayed until Finley sold the team.

But Burrell's life was just beginning. He went into the music business, called himself MC Hammer, and did pretty well. I was happy for him. He was a nice young man.

So were a lot of the other kids who served as batboys and batgirls on the teams I played for over the years. For a youngster who loved baseball, it didn't get any better than being in that position.

We always appreciated how dedicated they were and how seriously they took their responsibilities, but we played pranks on them just like we did on our teammates. Not the girls, just the boys.

If a batboy was sitting in the dugout waiting for the game to start, we might tell him to go into the clubhouse to fetch the key to the batter's box. The guys in the clubhouse, in on the joke, would tell him the key was at the batting cage. The players there would say, "You just missed the guy who took the key back to the clubhouse." When the batboy got back there, sweating and out of breath, he was told the key had been taken to the dugout for the start of the game. The poor kid ran all over the place looking for that elusive key.

Another time, we sent a batboy into the clubhouse to get the pitcher a box of curveballs.

One time during a rain delay, one of the players asked one of the batboys who was sitting in the dugout staying dry, "What happens if the rain washes out the foul lines and we can't see them? The umpires won't be able to tell if the ball is fair or foul. You need to cover up the lines so we can see them."

The kid nodded, grabbed an armful of towels, and started to lay them down end to end on the white lines. He was about halfway done when the rain stopped.

Whenever we pulled one of those pranks, all the players came over afterward to explain to the youngster that they had played a joke on him, praised him for being a team player, for following orders no matter how difficult it was, and presented him with an autographed team ball.

I didn't, however, get to spend much time with the batboys for the A's or anybody else in the Oakland organization. I appeared in only 15 games for the A's before the season ended.

When it came time to negotiate a new contract with Finley, it didn't take long. I figured I deserved a modest raise. After all, in my short stay, I won three games for him, two with home runs and one with a base hit. So I asked for a $5,000 raise.

His answer: "Do you want your release?"

My answer: "Yes."

Finley hung up and that was the last time I ever talked to him.

## TORONTO BLUE JAYS

Two weeks later, I got a call from Peter Bavasi, one of Buzzie's sons, who had become general manager of the Blue Jays, an expansion team. He wanted me to come to Toronto and help get his new club started.

When I said I would like to, Finley and Bavasi worked out a trade, sending me to the Blue Jays for minor league infielder Mike Weathers and cash.

So I joined a second Canadian team, and had a good year. Even though I played in only 132 games that season, 1977, I led the team in home runs with 19, and tied for most RBIs with 64.

When I made the All-Star team, Finley called Bavasi and demanded $25,000 in compensation for my success on the field. No way, said Bavasi, who reminded Finley that he was the one who called Bavasi and asked him to take me off his hands. Bavasi never gave Finley a penny.

I had some good days with the Blue Jays, but the one that meant the most to me was played in September in Yankee Stadium. We beat the Yankees, 19-3, our third baseman, Roy Howell, went 5-for-6 with nine RBIs, Jim Clancy got a complete-game victory, and I got my 1,000th career RBI. Good day for the Blue Jays.

In 1977, playing again in Canada for his second American League team, Ron led the Blue Jays in home runs, tied for the most RBIs, and made the All-Star team.

Another game from that season also stands out in my mind, but it's not a pleasant memory.

I was in the lineup as the designated hitter one afternoon in Toronto. The first time up, I foul tipped a ball into the catcher's glove for strike three. The second time up, I struck out on three pitches without swinging even once. The third time up, I tried to hold up on a pitch, but the ball hit my bat and rolled maybe 3 feet fair in front of home plate. The catcher scooped it up and tagged me out before I could run to first. In three at-bats, I had hit the ball a total of 3 feet.

As I was walking back to the dugout, it was quiet, enabling a fan near the dugout to be clearly heard as he shouted, "Designated *what?*"

All the fans in the area started to laugh. That pissed me off big time, but, as I sat down and thought about the kind of day I was having, I had to laugh along with the crowd and concede that the fan had asked a fair question. Boy, did I stink that day.

I often took one or two of my three boys to the ballpark because I thought it was a great experience for them. They would often help the clubhouse man in the visiting locker room clean up before and after games. It gave them a chance to be involved and hang around the players.

One night, we were playing the Baltimore Orioles when Kenny Singleton was on their team. The kids knew him because we had been teammates years earlier on the Expos.

On this particular night, I drove in two runs late in the game and we won. In the clubhouse afterward, my son Mike, 14 by then, was picking up towels and cleaning shoes when one of the Oriole pitchers loudly said, "I hate Fairly and, the next time I face him, I'm going to knock him on his ass."

Kenny walked over to the pitcher and quietly said, "Not so loud. That kid over there is Ron's son. Next time you face Ron, why don't you make better pitches to him."

Kenny was one of my kids' favorite players. Mine, too.

Another favorite was "The Rooster," Doug Rader. I played against him for 10 years before we became teammates with the Blue Jays.

One day, my kids were at the ballpark shagging fly balls during batting practice. They knew the rules I had for them to do that. Because of their age, they were not allowed to stand on the infield during batting practice because the balls are hit too hard for them to handle at such a close distance.

But on this day, 7-year-old Patrick, my youngest, was standing next to Doug at third base when batting practice started. He told Doug about my rule, but the third baseman replied, "Your dad is an idiot. You can stay here, but watch your lips because someone is liable to hit a ball at you, and you want to protect your mouth."

Just then, a line drive was ripped straight at Patrick. Fortunately, with the reflexes and experience of a third baseman, Doug was able to back-hand the ball an inch from Patrick's face.

"Didn't you see that ball?" Doug said.

"No, I was looking at you," Patrick told him.

"Your dad was right," said Doug, a little shaken by the thought of what might have happened. "Get in the outfield where you belong. You're the idiot for listening to me."

Years later, Doug was managing the Texas Rangers and I was an announcer for the Angels. I brought Patrick, then 13, to the ballpark so he could be the batboy for the Rangers.

Doug called Patrick into his office and told him he needed help filling out his lineup card for the game. After discussing it for a few minutes with my son, Doug wrote in the player positions and the batting order.

On the way home after the game, Patrick told me, "Dad, Doug said he didn't know who to play tonight and wanted me to make out the lineup card for him, so I did."

To this day, Patrick still thinks he's the one who put together the lineup that night.

I can't think about the Blue Jays without thinking about my dad and my grandfather and two home runs I hit. They gave me a feeling of intense pride and satisfaction, a lasting tribute to two of the most precious people in my life.

My grandfather, Paul Van Loan, the musical director who worked with Sonja Henie, knew very little about baseball. That was obvious to anyone who heard him tell his buddies all the time that I could hit a home run any time I wanted to. He said the reason I didn't hit a ton of home runs was because I didn't want to embarrass the pitchers.

That, of course, was ridiculous. If I could have hit a home run any time I wanted to, I would have homered every time up. The heck with the pitchers. But my dear grandfather never changed his story.

I was with the Dodgers in Pittsburgh the morning I got word that my grandfather had passed away. In my first at-bat, I hit a home run. Now, there was nothing unusual about that ... or was there?

Most of the home runs I hit in my career were to right and right center. Very, very few went to left field. It was 365 feet down the left field line in Forbes Field. I hit the ball pretty well, but I didn't hit it that well. I thought the ball would slice into our bullpen, well short of the fence. Instead, the ball kept going and going and going, sailing over the fence between the scoreboard and the foul pole. I know what it feels like to get bat on ball for a home run and I just didn't hit it that hard. All I could think of was that the ball was carrying really well that day.

Or maybe my grandpa knew what he was talking about. Maybe I really could hit a home run when I really wanted to.

It happened again, when I was with Toronto. My father played professional baseball for 11 years, and he taught me just about everything I know about baseball. The first game I played after he died was against the Angels in Anaheim. It was late in the game and the score was tied. With Paul Hartzell pitching for the Angels, I smacked a home run. This wasn't like the one in Pittsburgh. This time, I got all of it. As soon as I hit it, I knew it was gone. We won, and my home run was the difference in the game.

Here's the really crazy part of this: I hit a home run the first time up after my grandfather passed away, but we lost the game. I hit a home run in the first game I played after my dad died and we won. The difference was, Dad knew when to hit it.

## CALIFORNIA ANGELS

After the 1977 season, Peter Bavasi gave me a two-year contract with a nice increase in pay. It was the only time in my career that I had a multiyear contract. But then, during that winter, he traded me to the Angels for two minor leaguers, Pat Kelly, a catcher, and Butch Alberts, who would be used as a designated hitter.

Peter made the trade with his father, Buzzie, the new general manager of the Angels. So, it was a nice reunion for me. I was back with Buzzie, and finally coming home to Southern California nearly a decade after I had left the Dodgers.

The Angels were loaded. They had players like Don Baylor, Joe Rudi, Brian Downing, and Bobby Grich. Their pitching was led by a pair of aces, Nolan Ryan and Frank Tanana.

That season, the one in which I turned 40, I had only 235 at-bats, but I did hit 10 home runs, and drove in 40. On a team with so much talent, I was happy I was able to contribute something.

But whenever I think of that year, I am overwhelmed with sadness. Not because my own career was winding down — I had had a good run. No, it's because I think of Lyman Bostock, someone whose career should have been just taking off.

Lyman, a nice guy and a great teammate, was given a $2.25 million, five-year contract when he signed with the Angels as a free agent in November 1977.

After 10 years, Ron came back to Southern California in 1978 to spend his final year in uniform as a California Angel.

With big money comes big expectations. Lyman understood that. When he got off to a horrible start, he felt like he was letting the team down. With the pressure of the new contract weighing on him, Lyman got only two hits in his first 38 at-bats, and was hitting just .147 at the end of his first month.

"The tension," he told reporters, "was so tight … I felt myself standing outside my body up there at the plate, then jumping back into it just before the pitch. Everything was just a big glare in front of my face."

Lyman offered to give his first month's salary back to Angels owner Gene Autry. Through Buzzie, Gene declined.

"What if you hit .600 next month? You're sure as hell not getting any more money out of me," Buzzie told him.

"It floored me," Buzzie later told the L.A. Times. "I never knew a

.200 hitter who didn't think he deserved a raise. I never heard of a ball-player wanting to give $40,000 away."

Undeterred by the Angels, Lyman gave his month's pay to charity.

Determined to earn the rest of his salary, he worked hard to again become the hitter who had batted .323, and then .336 in his two previous seasons, both with the Minnesota Twins. By late September, Lyman's bat was back, his average up to .296.

With the season winding down, we were in Chicago to play the White Sox.

After a day game, Lyman went to visit his uncle, Ed Turner, in Gary, Indiana. The two were in a car along with two ladies Turner was driving home from dinner at his house. They were stopped at a light when Leonard Smith, the estranged husband of Barbara Smith, the woman sitting next to Lyman in the back seat, pulled up, jumped out, and fired a shotgun blast into the back of Turner's car, striking Lyman in the head.

He was rushed to a hospital, where he passed away fewer than three hours later.

At the ballpark the next day, we all stood around in the clubhouse, tears in our eyes. We didn't take batting practice, and nobody wanted to play the game.

"We're professionals," our manager, Jim Fregosi, told us, "and this is our business. We'll play this game like it should be played, though right now, the team is secondary. A man has lost his life, and a good friend is gone."

We played the game and won, 7-3, but there were no smiles, no high fives afterward. Like Fregosi said, we were professionals. We had a job to do, and we did it.

The Angels had only six games left in that season. I had just six games left in my career. I would retire at the end of the 1978 season at the age of 40. Earlier that month, I had commemorated the 20th anniversary of my first major league home run, Sept. 12, 1958, by hitting my last home run on Sept. 12, 1978.

I had come full circle on a journey that fulfilled all my dreams, and I loved every minute of it.

It was time to start a new journey.

# 13

## A Game Full
## of Unforgettables

I N MY HALF-CENTURY in baseball, both on the field and in the broadcast booth, I've had the good fortune to spend invaluable time with some of the greatest players to ever plant their cleats on a baseball field, some of the cleverest managers who have ever made out a lineup card, and some of the most colorful characters, whose mere presence enriched the game.

I've talked about many of them, but here are some more whose names still fill me with awe, bring a smile to my face, or generate feelings of profound respect.

## TED WILLIAMS

One day during my season with the Blue Jays, I was getting ready to take the field at Fenway Park when I was told Ted Williams was in the crowd.

Even though he had long since retired, he shook me up just by being there.

"Damn," I thought, "I've got to bear down today. Ted's watching me play."

That's how much he got in my head, even when he wasn't in uniform. I was thinking that I've got the greatest left-handed hitter who ever stood at the plate watching me hit. I'd better do something.

Fortunately, I had a good day, getting three hits.

Ted was not only the best I ever saw, but the most dominating person I've ever met, and I've been around some pretty powerful, big names. If you put him in a room with the top 75 executives in this country, within half an hour, he'd be in charge.

Yes, Ted was definitely opinionated. But I thought he had good ideas, and he was good at articulating them.

If Ted intimidated others, he himself was never intimidated. Not even when facing the greatest pitchers of his era.

Not even when facing the possibility of death in the scariest of all situations, military combat.

Ted served as a Marine fighter pilot in both World War II and the Korean War. World War II ended before he could get into combat, but he saw plenty of action in Korea, flying 39 combat missions. His plane was hit by enemy fire on at least three missions.

The most dramatic, described in a story published by the Marine Corps Association & Foundation, occurred on Feb. 16, 1953, when Ted's F9F Panther jet wobbled in to Suwon Air Base, 20 miles south of Seoul, South Korea, with smoke and fire streaming from it, the plane too low for the pilot to eject. As if that wasn't bad enough, there was an explosion on the underbelly of the aircraft as it zeroed in on the runway. The plane made a wheels-up belly landing, and skidded for a mile on the tarmac, smoke and sparks spreading over the airstrip. When the plane finally came to a halt, the nose burst into flames. Ted blew off the cockpit canopy, pulled his 6-foot-3-inch frame out of the wreckage, and jumped free.

Bob Kennedy, the longtime, major league player, manager, scout, and front-office executive, served in Korea with Ted, and was there when his plane came in aflame.

To Kennedy, it appeared there was no way to get that plane down in one piece. But somehow, some way, with a combination of courage, concentration, control, and luck, he brought it in.

So, when the jet fighter finally came to a complete stop, did Ted close his eyes, take a deep breath, permit himself to smile, and allow his heart to fill with the joy of being alive?

Not Ted. He hurriedly confronted the officers and medical personnel rushing toward him, according to Kennedy, and, in a fashion only Ted could muster in that situation, gave an order.

"Get me another plane," he said. "This damn one doesn't work very well. I want to go back up there and get that bleepity-bleep North Korean who shot my plane down."

"No way," he was told. "By the time you get back up there, he'll be somewhere over Manchuria."

"I don't give a shit," said Ted. "I'll find him."

By the time he left Korea, Ted had won three Air Medals. And he had impressed a fellow serviceman, a pretty good flier himself — his operations officer and frequent wingman, Maj. John Glenn. He would become the first American astronaut to orbit Earth, and a U.S. senator from Ohio.

Because he was such a good pilot, because he always put love of country ahead of love of baseball, Ted missed nearly five full seasons with the Red Sox in his prime.

He averaged 172 hits and 32 home runs in the years he played up to age 35, so if you figure another five years at those average numbers, he would have had 3,514 career hits and 681 home runs.

But opposing teams didn't need numbers to define Ted. Just watching him at the plate was enough to make them proceed with extreme caution.

In one game, Ted came up with the bases loaded, two outs, and his team trailing by two runs. The opposing manager intentionally walked him. The manager didn't want to give Ted the chance to get a hit that would drive in two and tie up the game. Instead, the strategy was, we'll give you one and try to get the next guy out.

A couple of managers would not even allow their pitchers to watch Ted take batting practice. They didn't want the pitcher to think, "*That's the guy I have to get out?*"

When Ted did make an out, he didn't handle it well. In an All-Star Game in 1959 at the L.A. Coliseum, Drysdale, facing Ted, decided to throw a spitter in on his hands. He threw the pitch exactly where he wanted, and Ted hit a towering fly ball to deep right center. The ball traveled about 430 feet before the right fielder caught it 10 feet short of the fence. That ended the inning. Don smiled and walked off the field.

Fast forward 10 years. I'm with the Dodgers in spring training in Vero Beach, standing in right field with Don, shagging fly balls during batting practice as we prepare to play the Washington Senators in an exhibition game at Holman Stadium.

Ted, retired for nine years, was managing the Senators. Their team bus pulled up in the right-field corner, the door opened, and the first man off was Ted. As he walked slowly toward the foul line, Don and I headed in his direction to say hello.

Before we had a chance to open our mouths, Ted spoke.

"What were you laughing at in the 1959 All-Star Game," he demanded to know, "when I popped up that horse-shit spitter you threw me?"

No "Hello." No "How is the family?"

Ted had made an out 10 years earlier in a game that didn't even count in the standings, and he was still bugged by the pitcher's reaction.

"Ted," Don replied, "I smiled because I got away with the pitch. When you hit it, I thought it was a home run, but it stayed in the park."

That caused Ted to laugh. "I just got under that SOB," he said, "but I had to ask you about the smile. And I had to ask you why in hell were you throwing me a spitter in an All-Star game?"

After he left, Don, his memory refreshed, told me, "I've had a lot of hitters take aggressive swings at my pitches, but that was the most vicious swing any batter ever took off me."

When it came to hitting, nobody understood the game of pitcher-versus-hitter better than Ted Williams. We had many conversations about that, and I never forgot several key points he made in explaining his philosophy: "You've got to get a good pitch to hit. You can't hit if you swing at tough pitches all the time. There is a good chance the pitcher will give you a better pitch to hit if you wait and only swing at the tough ones when you have two strikes on you."

Don't swing at the first pitch the first time up in the game. Because the information you get is more important than whether the pitch is a ball or a strike. You have to know how hard the pitcher is throwing that day. That tells you how quick you have to be with your hips. The quicker you get your hips out of the way, the quicker your hands can work.

Ted once asked me who was the toughest pitcher in the National League for me to hit. I told him it was Juan Marichal. "He gets me out just about any way he wants to," I said. "He has a good fastball, curve, slider, and change-up."

"Why do you let him get you out with all of his pitches?" Ted said. "Take a couple of them away from him. Change the odds by looking for something coming to the plate that is fast, like the fastball and slider, or look for something soft like the curve or change. Don't try to hit all of his pitches, just two of them. That improves your chances against him. Let the pitcher figure out which two you're looking for."

His theory worked. I started to have more success against Marichal.

It was fascinating to hear his analysis of a pitcher-hitter confrontation. As an example, he mentioned a pitcher who he knew would throw him 19 pitches in a typical game.

"That's what he's averaged when we have faced each other over the last six years," said Ted. "Of the 19 pitches, he will throw three change-ups, but he can't throw one for a strike. He'll throw nine fastballs, but only four will be strikes, seven curves, and four will be strikes.

"After my first two at-bats against him, I subtracted how many fast-balls, curves, and change-ups he had thrown me. It gave me better odds what to expect on my third and fourth time at bat. Is it time for the fastball to show up, or the off-speed pitch? What are the odds in the next two or three pitches that I will get one of those to hit? Odds above

75 to 90 percent are very good.

"That's the difference between guessing and having a real good idea what kind of pitch is coming.

"I looked for that pitch and, if, sure enough, there it was, I was ready for it. I was right a helluva lot more times than I was wrong. Thank God you're dealing with the dumbest SOB on the field, and that's the pitcher."

Hall of Fame pitcher Bob Lemon, who won 207 games in a 13-year career with the Cleveland Indians, was never comfortable pitching to Ted.

"When I pitched against the Red Sox and Ted was on deck," Lemon said, "I tried to concentrate on the batter, but all I could hear was the grinding, squeaking sound Ted made with rosin, squeezing the handle of the bat. I was thinking more about him than the guy in the batter's box.

"There's another thing he did that annoyed me. Every other hitter in the league took their time getting into the batter's box, waiting for their name to be announced to the crowd, but not Ted. He was always standing at the plate, waiting for me to get back on the rubber after the last batter. He couldn't wait to hit off me.

"Every time I pitched to him, as I was in the middle of my windup, I had the feeling he knew what I was going to throw. Getting Ted Williams out was like playing poker with someone who knows your hole cards. I never surprised or fooled him."

One year at the All-Star Game, Ted explained his theories about hitting to all the other players. Lou Boudreaux was the player/manager for the Indians, and he was listening. When the Indians faced the Red Sox right after the All-Star Game, Boudreaux held a team meeting, and told his pitchers how he wanted them to pitch to Williams. "First, we are going to throw him nothing but slop, change-ups and slow curves, the slower the better. When we get two strikes on him, we're going to bust him with a good fastball in on his hands."

One of his pitchers, "Jittery" Joe Berry, raised his hand and said, "Skipper, I have one question. How do you get two strikes on that SOB?"

Left-hander Hank Aguirre, who later went on to pitch for the Dodgers, faced Ted for the first time coming out of the bullpen as a rookie a few days after joining the Indians. Aguirre threw Ted sidearm curveballs low and away, and struck him out.

Before the next game, Aguirre went to Ted and said, "Hi, Mr. Williams, I'm Hank Aguirre. I pitched against you yesterday and struck you out. Would you please sign the ball?"

Aguirre's teammates were all back in their own clubhouse snickering. They knew Ted, and had persuaded the naïve young pitcher to ask for the autograph just to see the reaction.

There was none at first. Ted simply nodded and signed.

Aguirre went back to the bullpen, got the call again in that series, went in to face Ted, and thought, "I know how to pitch him. I'll just throw him the sidearm curve low and away. No problem."

On the first pitch, Ted hit a line drive over the right-center field fence for a home run. The ball took off like it was hit with a 4-iron, and landed about 75 feet beyond the fence.

As he rounded third, Ted yelled out to Aguirre, "Have your teammates get that ball and I'll sign it, too."

## GEORGE STEINBRENNER

Steinbrenner, who owned the Yankees for 37 years until his death in 2010 at age 80, demanded excellence from his players and respect from his employees. When Lou Piniella was managing the Seattle Mariners, and I was a broadcaster in Seattle, he told me a few stories about his days playing for Steinbrenner's Yankees.

When his plane would arrive in New York, the word spread around the Yankee Stadium offices that The Eagle had landed. That meant Steinbrenner was at the airport.

A limousine company was always on call to pick him up and bring him to the stadium. One day, walking into the baggage claim area, he was greeted by a driver who was shorter than 5 feet, with a slight build. Steinbrenner had to help the driver put the luggage into the trunk of the car.

He asked the driver if he knew the shortcut to Yankee Stadium. The driver shook his head no.

Exasperated, Steinbrenner ordered the driver to get in the back seat. He got behind the wheel and drove himself to the stadium.

He was red-faced with anger by the time he got there, demanding to know who had pulled the prank on him, putting him in a situation where he had to handle his own luggage and do the driving himself. When he didn't get any answers, he threatened to fire the entire front office.

Steinbrenner eventually calmed down, but the muffled giggling continued in offices all over the stadium.

One summer night in 1987, the Yankees were playing the Angels in Anaheim. Tommy John was pitching for New York, and Don Sutton for the Angels.

During the game, the Yankee clubhouse man brought a phone out to the dugout, handed it to Yankee Manager Lou Piniella. "George wants to talk to you."

Steinbrenner was calling from New York.

"I don't want to talk to him now," Piniella said. "We're playing a game."

With a desperate look on his face, the clubhouse man said, "Lou, if you don't take the call, I get fired."

Shaking his head in disgust, Piniella took the call.

Lou: Hi, George, what can I do for you?

George: What can you do for *me?* You can start by complaining to the umpire about Sutton. Whose side are you on? Sutton is out there cheating, scuffing up the baseballs, and you're not saying one word. You know what he is doing. Why aren't you out there complaining?

Lou: George, what's the score?

George: We're winning 1-0, but what difference does that make?

Lou: Who's pitching for us?

George: Tommy John.

Lou: Who do you think taught Sutton how to scuff up baseballs? It was Tommy John, and right now, he's doing a better job of scuffing than Sutton is. He's got a shutout going. Do you want the umpires to go out and check him, too?

Click. George hung up the phone.

Another time, Lou was called into Steinbrenner's office when George was upset with his managing philosophy.

George: Lou, you're killing me with the decisions you're making on the field. I know a lot about this, believe me, and you're driving me crazy. You take a pitcher out when you should leave him in, and you leave him in when you should take him out.

Lou: OK, fine, from now on, you make the call. When I go to the mound, I'll look at you up in your suite, and you give me thumbs up to leave the pitcher in and thumbs down to take him out.

George: Fine. Thumbs up, leave him in, thumbs down, you take him out. It can't be that tough.

Two days later, with the Yankees in a close game, Lou went out to the mound. He looked up at Steinbrenner in his suite, waiting for a thumb up or thumb down. The Yankee owner seemed frozen. He was just standing there, staring.

Lou continued to look for the signal. The home plate umpire, getting annoyed about the delay, came to the mound to speed up the game.

Lou kept looking, and finally, Steinbrenner reacted. He stuck his thumb up. But then, he jammed it down. Back up, back down.

Lou, totally confused, left the pitcher in the game, and the Yankees wound up winning.

Afterward, he went to Steinbrenner's office for a clarification. "George," said Lou, "I didn't understand your thumb signals. Let's go over the signs again. Thumb up means keep the pitcher in the game, and thumb down means take him out. What does thumb up, thumb down, thumb up, thumb down mean?"

"I don't know, but dammit," George growled, "it better be right."

## YOGI BERRA

At 5 feet 7 inches, Yogi wasn't very big, but he put up big numbers. He played 18 years with the Yankees, plus a brief return for four games with the Mets at 40. Primarily a catcher, he had a career batting average of .285 with 358 home runs and 1,430 RBIs, was the American League MVP three times (1951, '54, and '55), appeared in 18 All-Star Games, and is, of course, a member of the Hall of Fame.

I've talked to pitchers who said Yogi was a tougher out than Mantle or Joe DiMaggio. Yogi would swing at pitches outside the strike zone, yet was tough to strike out. In 8,359 career plate appearances, he struck out only 414 times. That's one strikeout for every 20 trips to the plate. Six times in his career, he had more home runs than strikeouts in a season.

Because Yogi became best known for all the funny things he said, some people today don't know just how great a player he was. Opposing pitchers weren't laughing when he stepped to the plate.

Who didn't like Yogi? Who wouldn't like a guy who wore a different golf shirt every day during spring training, and when someone commented that he must like them a lot because he'd worn a different color every day, said, "Yeah, I have one in every color but navy brown."

Navy brown?

When I was with the Montreal Expos, we were taking batting practice one day and Yogi was standing behind the batting cage, watching us hit. Tom Seaver walked by and said, "Yogi, what time is it?"

"Right now?"

"No," Seaver answered, "tell me what time it was 20 minutes ago, and I'll figure it out."

Yogi died in 2015 at 90, but his Yogi-isms live on. He said:

- "Always go to other people's funerals. Otherwise they won't go to yours."
- "You'd better cut the pizza into four pieces, because I'm not hungry enough to eat six."
- "Never answer an anonymous letter."
- And, his most repeated Yogi-isms, "When you see a fork in the road, take it," and "It ain't over till it's over."

People who heard Yogi's expressions and underestimated his intelligence learned the hard way that, when it came to the game he loved, he was as sharp as anyone on the field.

As a catcher, he always talked to hitters when they came to the plate — about their golf game or the weather or the crowd or whatever else came to mind.

One spring, in a game between the Dodgers and the Yankees with Yogi behind the plate, I grounded out my first two times up. But while I was standing at the plate during my second at-bat, Yogi mentioned that the wind was blowing in from right field.

My third time up, I moved up in the batter's box, looking for a fast-ball I could keep away from the wind by hitting it up the middle or to left field. So, when I reached the plate, I stepped up a few inches.

"Ron," said Yogi, "how come you're not standing in the same place you were the first two times up?"

Yogi might not have had a great formal education, but he learned every nuance of the game, like when hitters made adjustments at the plate, and he made sure his pitchers then made adjustments of their own.

Years ago, the New York chapter of the Baseball Writers' Association gave Yogi an award. The annual awards dinner was held at Toots Shor's, the famous Manhattan restaurant. Along with a plaque, Yogi was given a beautiful, expensive table clock. After the event, Yogi was carrying it out of the restaurant when a drunk passing by bumped into him.

"Hey, watch where you're going," Yogi said.

The drunk looked at Yogi, looked at the clock, and said, "Why don't you carry a watch like everyone else."

### MANAGER GIL HODGES

Gil Hodges made his first appearance in a Dodgers uniform at the age of 19. But after appearing in just one game, he left to enter the military when the planet became engulfed in World War II.

When he returned to civilian life, the Dodgers sent him a contract for the 1947 season. Gil's real name was Gilbert Raymond Hodge. But the secretary who typed up the contract misspelled his last name, adding an "s," making it Hodges instead of Hodge. Gil was so elated at the chance to trade his military uniform for a baseball uniform that he sent the contract back anyway, not wanting to risk the possibility that the Dodgers, given a second chance, might decide to rescind the contract.

And so began an 18-year big league career as one of the premier first baseman in either league. He then went on to a successful, but all-too-brief career as a manager.

At 6 feet 1 inch and 200 pounds, Gil was an exceptionally strong man with very large hands. When we compared our hands, my fingers were two joints short of his. He could make anyone say "uncle" with just two fingers. He would grab you by the wrist with his thumb and index finger, and sink that index finger into your wrist until you tapped out.

But Gil was certainly not a bully. He was soft-spoken and one of the gentlest men I've ever met. It would take a lot to get him mad, but if someone did, they were suddenly dealing with an entirely different person.

That Gil Hodges emerged more often in his managerial days. One season during his years as skipper of the Washington Senators, the team had fallen into a slump that reached a low point when they lost on a walk-off home run by Dick McAuliffe in Detroit, the Senators' second walk-off loss in a row to the Tigers.

Gil couldn't stand it anymore. He told his players that they had 15 minutes to get dressed and get out of the clubhouse, and he wasn't kidding. Some players didn't even bother to shower, instead grabbing their clothes and going to their hotel to clean up.

Only four or five players remained when Gil came into the clubhouse. Rather than chairs, there were wooden stools in front of the lockers. When he entered, there was a stool in his way that he picked up and slammed on the floor. When it didn't break, he got angrier still. He picked up the stool, broke its legs off, grabbed one of the broken legs, and snapped it in half like you'd break a small stick. Then he grabbed another leg with his massive hands, and snapped that one in half as well.

The sight and sounds generated by their raging manager scared the hell out of the remaining players. One hid in his locker stall, and the others got out of Dodge as fast as they could. They had found out just how strong their manager was in an incident they wouldn't soon forget.

The next day, Gil was back to his normal self. He held a short, routine clubhouse meeting, announced the starting lineup, and left, his demeanor as calm as ever.

In 1969, the Mets, with Gil leading the way as manager, became the Amazin' Mets, winning the World Series just seven years after their dreadful debut. In a July doubleheader at Shea Stadium, they were getting thoroughly whipped by the Astros, losing the opener 16-3, then falling behind in the nightcap, 8-0, in the third inning.

The eighth run had come in on a double by catcher Johnny Edwards that got by Cleon Jones in left field.

At that point, Gil came out of the dugout and appeared to be walking to the mound. That's what the announcers told the crowd, but Gil walked past pitcher Nolan Ryan, and turned left.

The Mets' shortstop, Buddy Harrelson, thought with some trepidation that the manager was coming after him, though he couldn't imagine why. He looked at Gil and pointed to his own chest, but Gil shook his head no, and walked past the shortstop as well.

Finally, Gil reached Jones while everybody was trying to figure out what the manager was doing in left field in the middle of an inning when it didn't appear the left fielder was hurt.

Gil, fuming because he felt Jones had not hustled after the ball hit by Edwards, told Jones that it appeared he was "nursing" his previously injured ankle. The left fielder assured his manager that was not the case, that he had not run at full speed because the grass was wet.

Gil, knowing the ankle wasn't the problem, told Jones to come with him. Gil turned and walked back to the dugout, his embarrassed and dejected left fielder following him. Ron Swoboda replaced him in left.

It wasn't as if Jones wasn't producing for the club. He had been 3-for-5 that day, and was leading the Mets with a .344 average.

But Gil was trying to make a point that lack of hustle was an unforgivable sin on his team. Whether it was breaking stools or breaking bad habits, he knew how to get his team's attention.

He certainly got his point across that day. After losing that second game, 11-5, the Mets went on a tear, finishing the regular season with a 45-19 record before going on to win the World Series.

Two-and-a-half years later, while in spring training in Florida with the Mets, Gil played 27 holes of golf in West Palm Beach with three of his coaches, Joe Pignatano, Rube Walker, and Eddie Yost.

Afterward, walking back to his hotel room, Gil collapsed. He died of a heart attack in less than an hour at a nearby hospital. Gil was just 47.

The baseball world lost a great man, and those of us who knew him lost a great friend.

## TOMMY LASORDA

As a manager, Tommy Lasorda won four pennants and two World Series in 20 years at the Dodgers helm, second only to Walt Alston in all those categories.

As a storyteller, Tommy is unequaled.

I first met him at Vero Beach in 1960 after he had retired as a player and was scouting for the Dodgers. I started listening to his stories back then, and have been entertained by him ever since.

While managing in the minor leagues, he had a pitcher who always seemed to develop arm problems about the sixth or seventh inning of close games. If the game wasn't tight, neither was the arm.

Understandably, Tommy was convinced there was nothing wrong with the pitcher's arm. The problem was in his head.

Sure enough, the next time the pitcher was in a close game, he began showing signs of discomfort in the seventh inning.

"Anything wrong? How do you feel?" Tommy asked when he came out to the mound.

"My arm hurts a little," said the pitcher.

"Does it hurt when you laugh?" Tommy asked.

"No," said the pitcher.

"Well, throw this next pitch, and then laugh," Tommy said.

"There are three kinds of players," he once told me. "Players who can make things happen on the field, players who would love to be able to make things happen, and players who wonder what happened."

Like Mickey Hatcher and Joe Ferguson in the story Tommy tells

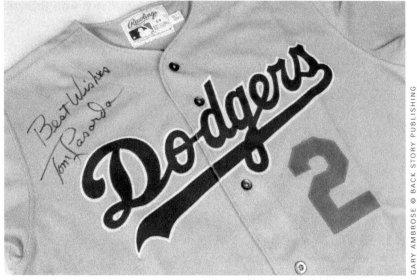

**Tommy Lasorda was a mediocre ballplayer, a terrific manager, and a master storyteller.**

about a game in which the Dodgers were on the field with two outs and a runner at third base. With Ferguson behind the plate as the catcher, the batter hit a ground ball to Hatcher at third. Normally, the third baseman, with two outs, would field the ball and throw it to first for the final out of the inning. The catcher would normally follow the batter down the first-base line in case of a bad throw.

Instead, Hatcher threw the ball to home plate where Ferguson, still standing there, caught it and tagged the runner coming in from third to end the inning.

When Hatcher came into the dugout, Tommy shouted, "What the hell is going on out there? Why did you throw the ball to the plate?"

"Tommy, I thought there was only one out," Hatcher told him.

Lasorda then turned to Ferguson and said, "Joe, why did you stay at home? Why didn't you back up first?"

"Tommy," replied Ferguson, "when you play with dummies, you have to think like a dummy."

In the clubhouse at Vero Beach, a sign on the wall read, "Soup of the Day," and underneath it was a large pot of soup.

One day, Tommy hollered across the locker room at outfielder Kenny

178

Landreaux, "What's the soup?"

Landreaux looked at the sign and hollered back, "of the day."

Landreaux didn't like people calling him by his first name — he preferred initials. He wanted everyone to call him "KT."

Tommy once asked him, "Why do you call yourself KT? Your name is Kenneth Francis Landreaux."

"Because I like the way it sounds," said Landreaux.

"But those are not your initials," insisted Tommy.

"So what?" said Landreaux. "What about the guy who decided water could be $H_2O$?"

## DANNY MURTAUGH

Danny Murtaugh was a Hall of Fame manager with the Pirates, winning two World Series with them in his 15 seasons as their skipper.

The Pittsburgh players learned there was no way to fool their manager because there was nothing they were going to come up with that he hadn't done himself back in his playing days as an infielder in the 1940s and early '50s.

Danny once told me about a spring training trip he took with a teammate. They drove to a race track in Miami and won around $400, a huge amount in those days.

When they left the track, it was time to celebrate. They went to a fancy Miami steakhouse and had a great meal, along with a lot to drink.

By the time they were done, it was late. Not wanting to get caught out after curfew, they decided to stay in a Miami motel, get up early in the morning, and drive back to camp.

Everything seemed to be going smoothly until Murtaugh walked into the lobby of the team hotel the next morning with a newspaper under his arm. Waiting for him was his manager.

"Good morning, skipper," said Murtaugh. "How are you today?"

"I'm fine," said the manager, "but where have you been?"

Thinking quickly, Murtaugh said with an innocent smile, "I got up early, went down the street, had breakfast, and read the paper."

"That's interesting," said the manager, his eyes narrowing, "because this morning at 3 a.m., a truck driver fell asleep at the wheel and drove his truck right through your room. We've been looking for you all night."

Oops.

Every baseball fan has seen a manager come out of his dugout and harangue an umpire about what the manager thinks is a bad call. But unless you're a lip reader, you can't always be sure what they are saying.

Especially if the manager is Danny Murtaugh.

Murtaugh loved to go on the field and argue with umpire Jocko Conlan. It got to the point where Jocko would get agitated merely seeing Murtaugh step out of his dugout.

In one series, the Pirate manager kept waiting and waiting for a controversial play involving Jocko so that he could get under the umpire's skin.

Finally, Murtaugh saw his chance when a Pirate base runner was thrown out trying to steal second. It was close, but the runner was clearly out.

Nevertheless, Murtaugh ran onto the field, heading for second base. When he reached Jocko, the umpire barked at him, "Get off the field you hard-headed Irishman. The play was not that close."

Murtaugh got in Jocko's face and calmly said, "I know you made the correct call and the runner was out."

Murtaugh pointed to the dirt where the base runner had been tagged out, held his hands about 3 feet apart and said, "It looked like the runner was out by about this much."

"Then why are you on the field?" asked the exasperated umpire. "Go back to the dugout where you belong."

Murtaugh took one step, spun around, and began jabbing his finger at Jocko.

There was only one way for the fans in the stands to interpret all this. They figured their manager was berating the umpire and they loved it, loudly cheering him on while vociferously booing the umpire.

"Here's another thing," Murtaugh told Jocko. "I think you're one of the best umpires in the league."

"Get out of here," Jocko, furious, yelled at Murtaugh.

With the entire ballpark in an uproar, the Pirate manager started to walk away again, then pivoted back one more time to say, "Jocko, you're the only umpire in the league who wears a bowtie. I salute you for that. I think all the umpires should wear bowties."

With that, Murtaugh, a big smile on his face, walked back to his dugout accompanied by a standing ovation from the fans. He had sent them a message that bad calls against the Pirates were not going to be tolerated.

Even if they were actually good calls.

One year in spring training, Murtaugh roomed with the traveling secretary to save the team money.

Most nights, Murtaugh went to bed early because he wanted to get up and get to the ballpark early. The traveling secretary stayed out late because he didn't have to get to the stadium until much later.

Sometimes, the traveling secretary would wake Murtaugh up when he came into the room in the wee hours, and the manager had a rough time going back to sleep. Finally, Murtaugh had had enough and decided to do something about it on a night the Pirates were staying in a hotel with a louvered door.

As usual, the arrival of the traveling secretary in the middle of the night awakened Murtaugh, but he kept his eyes shut until the traveling secretary had fallen asleep. Then Murtaugh quietly got out of bed, went to his coaches' room, and woke them up. They went back to Murtaugh's room with a large metal trash can filled to the top with junk. They tied a rope from the outside door knob to a nearby palm tree, placed the trash can next to the louvered door, lit the trash, and fanned the smoke into the room.

Once the room began to fill with smoke, Murtaugh and the coaches hollered to the traveling secretary to wake up and get out of bed because the hotel was on fire.

Awakened and panicked, he jumped out of bed and tried to open the door, but he couldn't because it was tied to the palm tree.

After a frantic few seconds, a chair came crashing through the window, followed by the traveling secretary who was greeted by a standing ovation from Murtaugh and his coaches.

It cost Murtaugh some money, but it was the last time the traveling secretary stayed out late.

## PRESTON GOMEZ

I have mentioned others in this chapter for their talent, their success, and their humor. I have included Preston Gomez for his heart. He was a great baseball man who, in addition to managing the Dodgers' Spokane farm team when I was there in 1960, also managed at the major league level as the skipper of the Padres, Astros, and Cubs.

Preston was also a third-base coach for the Dodgers. In my opinion, he was the best the team ever had. When he was relaying signs from the manager, no one was ever able to steal them. Why? Because Preston had a different set of signs for everyone in the starting lineup. I had the same signs for 10 years. There was no way any team could keep track of which sign belonged to which player.

But the reason I have singled out Preston, who was Cuban-born, was not for what he did on the field in front of the fans and the media, but for what he did away from public view for the Latin ballplayers. They were a long way from home, in a different country, experiencing a different culture, eating different food, and speaking a different language

Today, if a player has a problem fitting in to what, for them, is a strange new world, teams address it right away. The players are supplied with an interpreter if they need one. Teams deploy staff members, if necessary, to show the players how to find an apartment, where to eat, and how to get to and from the ballpark.

Back then, Preston was often a one-man welcome wagon in helping players from Latin countries acclimate to the major leagues.

When right-hander Luis Sanchez was called up from the minors by the Angels, the team was about to embark for Milwaukee. As one of the team's broadcasters, I was part of the traveling party. When we arrived at the hotel around midnight, the players went to their rooms to wait for their luggage to arrive from the airport. When Preston, then the Angels' third-base coach, came down to get his luggage, he noticed that Sanchez, a native of Venezuela, was still in the lobby.

After spending a few minutes talking to the pitcher, Preston realized something that would have shocked anyone unfamiliar with the conditions some Latin players lived in back home — Sanchez had never been on an elevator before.

When the luggage arrived, Preston got on the elevator with Sanchez and took him to his room.

The next morning, Preston called the room three or four times, but got no answer. When knocked on the door, Sanchez opened it.

"Why didn't you answer the phone," Preston asked him.

"I heard this ringing sound," Sanchez said, "but didn't know what it was."

He didn't know how to use a telephone.

Preston ate breakfast and lunch with Sanchez every day, and taught him how to order food from the menu. In the afternoon, Preston took Sanchez to the ballpark for every game until the pitcher learned how to get there on his own.

Sanchez wound up pitching for the Angels out of the bullpen for five years. He won 28 games and had 27 saves for them, relying on a good sinking fastball and decent control. He finished up his career with two seasons in Japan.

Preston didn't limit his support only to active players.

Outfielder Sandy Amoros made the most memorable play of Game 7 of the 1955 World Series between the Dodgers and the Yankees.

With the Dodgers leading, 2-0, at Yankee Stadium heading into the bottom of the sixth inning, Alston, having hit for second baseman Don Zimmer in the top half of the inning, moved Jim Gilliam from left field to second and sent Amoros into left. It proved to be Alston's smartest move of the game.

With runners on first and second and nobody out, Yogi Berra sliced a ball toward the left-field corner that appeared to be headed for extra bases. Amoros, who was playing the left-handed hitting Berra in left center, got a great jump on the ball and raced toward the seats near the foul pole. Amoros, who was left-handed and therefore wore his glove on his right hand, stretched his right arm out as far as he could, caught the ball, spun around, and threw a strike to Pee Wee Reese, who was near the third-base line. Reese, in turn, fired the ball to Hodges at first base to double up Gil McDougald, who couldn't get back to the bag in time.

The Dodgers hung on for a 2-0 victory.

If Gilliam had still been in left, the catch probably couldn't have been made. He was fast, but he couldn't have matched Amoros' blazing speed. And because Gilliam was right-handed, he would have had to stretch his gloved left hand across his body to reach the ball, probably leaving him short of his target. If Amoros had not caught that ball, it might have caromed around the left-field corner, enabling both runners to score and tie the game.

And the defining moment in Brooklyn Dodger history, the franchise's first world championship, might not have happened.

Amoros' last season in the big leagues was 1960, after which he fell on hard times. He moved back to Cuba, but refused an offer by Prime Minister Fidel Castro to manage a Cuban summer league team. Anyone who turned down the Cuban dictator did so at their own peril. In Amoros' case, Castro confiscated his ranch and took everything Amoros had, but forbade him from leaving the country.

In 1967, Castro finally allowed Amoros to return to the United States. It was around the first of September when major league teams could expand their rosters. Amoros needed just a few days on a big league roster to be eligible for the Major League Baseball players' pension plan. Dodgers President Walter O'Malley, remembering what Amoros had done for the team more than a decade earlier and still considering him part of the family, offered him a contract.

We were in Houston to play the Astros when Amoros arrived. Preston, who could certainly relate to leaving Cuba, met his countryman at the airport, and brought him to the team hotel.

The next morning, I happened to meet Preston in the lobby, and he told me about Amoros' condition. He was skinny, had no money, and his clothes were old, torn, and dirty.

Preston was waiting to take Amoros to buy him new clothes. Preston understood how looking successful could instill confidence in a ballplayer. Preston himself always wore a suit and tie when he was with the team.

When Amoros met us, I saw what Preston was talking about. Amoros didn't look good, but he did have a big smile on his face.

I went along to the men's store, where we bought Amoros slacks, sport coats, two pairs of shoes, and accessories. We wanted him to feel good about himself when he walked into our clubhouse. I know Preston went back to the store a few days later and bought some more things for Amoros, and added still more items to his wardrobe when we got back to L.A.

He was certainly not in any condition to go into a game, but all the players went out of their way to make him feel welcome and part of the team. He came out every day, one of the first to arrive at the ballpark, that smile never leaving his face.

Amoros remained on the team enough days to qualify for the pension plan. He wasn't on our team long, but, for a brief, shining period, he was a kid again, wearing a Dodgers uniform, basking in his memories.

It was Preston who first put that smile on the face of Amoros, setting the mood for his return to the clubhouse, making sure he was dressed for the occasion.

All managers and coaches are concerned with a player's arm, legs, glove, bat, attitude, and work ethic. But the really good ones, like Preston, are also concerned with a player's dignity.

# 14

## Trading My Bat
## for a Microphone

BRANCH RICKEY SAID he'd rather trade a player a year too soon than a year too late.

I thought about that in the spring of 1979 when I got a call from Gene Autry, who had made his fortune singing and acting as "The Cowboy" before becoming the owner of an expansion team named the Los Angeles Angels, and forming Golden West Broadcasters. It expanded to include two TV and eight radio stations.

My old teammate, Don Drysdale, was part of the Angels' broadcast crew along with Dick Enberg, a consummate pro. Gene asked if I would be interested in joining them. In addition, he offered to make me the sportscaster on the evening news on TV station KTLA, Channel 5 in Los Angeles. Gene also owned radio station KMPC, flagship of the Angels network.

I felt like I could still play, could still handle a good fastball, but for how long? I was 40 years old, and an opportunity like the one Gene was dangling in front of me, a new career in my hometown and the chance to stay in the game I loved indefinitely, might not come my way again.

That's when Mr. Rickey's words popped in my head. I decided I would rather retire a year too soon than a year too late.

So, I accepted the offer and hung up my glove.

## ANAHEIM

I enjoyed working for Gene Autry, who had become a very successful businessman.

We played our spring training games in Palm Springs, and sometime, Gene would bring some of his Hollywood buddies into our booth. Phil Harris, who lived in the Palm Springs area, was one of my favorites. He was a comedian, movie star, and was married to actress Alice Faye. Whenever he visited the radio booth, he kind of took over the broadcast — I was more like his straight man who also had to keep the listeners updated about the game. This is how I remember one such broadcast.

Ron: We're in the bottom half of the fourth inning, and the Angels are leading the Indians by a score of 2 to 1. We have a special guest with us today, an old friend of Gene Autry, who lives here in the Palm Springs area, Mr. Phil Harris. Hi Phil, and welcome to our booth. How have you been?

Phil: Thanks Ron, I feel great and I always look forward to the Angels coming to Palm Springs. It gives me a chance to watch all these great athletes working out and getting ready for the season.

Ron: Rod Carew will lead things off for the Angels in the fourth inning. Rod singled to left his first time up, and the first pitch to Carew is outside, ball one. Phil now that you've retired from show business, what do you do to stay healthy?

Phil: Ron, I have found out that the most important meal of the day for me is breakfast.

Ron: Why is that?

Phil: Because if I'm not home by then, Alice really gets pissed.

Ron: The next pitch to Carew is outside, two balls and no strikes. (I momentarily switched off the mic to recover.)

Another broadcast visit by Phil also challenged my concentration.

Ron: We have a 2-2 tie as Bobby Grich leads things off for the Angels here in the fifth inning. It's good to have our old friend Phil Harris with us again on the Angels broadcast. Phil, welcome back. How have you been and what have you been up to lately?

Phil: Ron, Alice and I have been doing some traveling, not a lot but some.

Ron: Grich takes the first pitch in the dirt, one ball no strikes. Phil, you must have traveled a great deal in your career, and I know what a great job you did entertaining thousands of people all over the world.

Phil: We really had a wonderful time entertaining the folks, and specially our men and women in the military. Ron, I've sailed around the world a couple of times and in my traveling I have found out one thing.

Ron: What's that?

Phil: You can get just as drunk on water as you can on land.

Listeners never knew what happened on the second pitch to Grich, because I was laughing so hard I missed it.

I knew Dick Enberg was a great announcer, but working with him on TV, I quickly found out how great a teacher he was as well. From him, I learned the best methods for preparing for a game. I learned a basic requirement for a baseball broadcaster — knowing how to keep score of the game. It's the universal shorthand for play-by-play. You'd be surprised how many players don't know how to keep score.

But the No. 1 thing Dick stressed was that, as the color man on the broadcast, I had to make sure I did not repeat what he had just said. "Tell me something different," he would say, "something the fans didn't see or previously hear."

Sometimes, doing the color is tougher than doing play-by-play, especially when an announcer describes the play as well as Dick did.

Playing major league baseball could be a humbling experience and, as I found out, so could announcing baseball games.

In my first spring training in the broadcast booth, I realized that exhibition games can be a nightmare. It might have been fun to live in a place like Dodgertown, doing morning workouts, playing four or five innings in the game, then having the rest of the day off. But when you are behind the microphone, you have to go the full nine innings and, in the latter stages of the game, you are dealing with the minor leaguers.

Approximately 50 players appear in a spring training game.

Many times, when substitutions were made, we were not given the names of some of the players. If a ball was hit to one of them, we couldn't say who it was, or anything else about them.

In 1980, announcer Bob Starr, a veteran of nearly a quarter-century doing play-by-play, was hired for the radio side of the Angel broadcasts, but also did some TV. Calling a spring game, he told his audience, "Now playing in center field is Kenny Campus. Out of the University of Oklahoma, he's 6 foot 1, and weighs 185 pounds. Kenny spells his last name with a 'C.' Next pitch, there's a lazy fly ball to center, Campus is under it, and has it for out No. 1."

When the inning was over, I asked Bob where he got that name.

"Ron," he said, "you always have to have a couple of names in your head you can use when you don't know who is on the field. I came up with three I could always go to. I used Kenny Campus, and I also used Sammy Jorgensen and Phil Miller. Kenny Campus was like saying 'Joe College,' Sammy Jorgensen sounded like a ballplayer's name, and Phil Miller is a close friend of mine who I have known since the third grade. Phil has no idea how many spring training games he has played."

As a play-by-play announcer, Bob preferred radio over television.

"An elementary school teacher who was talking about baseball asked his students, 'Which is better, radio or television?'" said Bob. "Every kid in the class said television because you can see the game. Every kid but one little boy, who said 'radio.' When the teacher asked him why, the kid said, 'Because the pictures are better.' In his mind, the announcer painted a better picture than the one he saw on the screen. You don't know how hard the wind is blowing in from right field until the announcer tells you. You can't tell how green the grass is, or how far a home run was hit until the announcer tells you.

"Television is a director's medium. You're controlled by what pictures are put on the screen. On radio, the announcer is the director. He knows where he's going to take the listener, and what storyline he wants to pursue. Many times on television, I've wanted to talk about someone or something, but I couldn't because the graphics for an advertiser appeared on the screen, and I had to read the commercial. On radio, I could finish my thought or my story, and then do the commercial."

Radio and television are both in the business of communication, but that doesn't mean that the communication is always great. In one game in which I was behind the microphone, the communication between the broadcast booth and the director was an embarrassing disaster.

It was a telecast of an Angels-Padres spring training game in Yuma, Arizona. Midway through, the director told the cameraman to zoom in on four people sitting directly behind home plate. The men were wearing coats and ties, and the woman was also nicely dressed. I had no idea who they were, so I didn't mention them on the air. The next inning, the director put them on camera again after each out, but still, nobody told me why they were in the spotlight.

So, between innings, I asked the guys in the video production truck.

Truck: Give me a minute and I'll let you know. ... It's the mayor.

Ron (on camera): Here at the game today, we would like to welcome the mayor of Yuma, and his staff who are sitting behind home plate. We hope he's enjoying the game.

Truck: No, no, Ron, it's the mayor of San Diego.

Ron: I'm sorry, fans, it's not the mayor of Yuma, but the mayor of San Diego. He and his staff came all the way here to Yuma to attend the game.

Truck: No, no, no, Ron, the lady is the mayor.

I was furious because I had been made to look like an unprepared fool. It doesn't matter who does what behind the scenes — if you are the person on the air, as far as the viewers are concerned, you own any screwup.

During a stretch when the Angels were not playing well, it started drizzling during a game. Bob Starr and I alerted KTLA so that the station could prepare for alternate programing if the rain intensified.

It did. About 15 minutes later, the rain increased from a drizzle to a downpour, and the weather radar showed it was going to last for at least an hour.

During the delay, KTLA ran a show starring The Three Stooges.

After an hour and a half, the rain stopped, the game resumed, and the Angels eventually won.

The next day, we found out that The Three Stooges had a higher rating than the game.

Humbling, indeed.

# LEARNING FROM THE MASTER

From all his decades on the air, one announcer made me understand a phenomenon I call the Vin Scully Rule of Baseball.

As an announcer, I would never start a story when there were two outs. The next pitch could end the inning, and I wouldn't be able to finish my story because the station would have to go to a commercial break. But whenever Vinny told a story, the phenomenon occurred. Everything slowed down. The batter stepped out of the box, or something got in his eye, the pitcher asked for a new ball, the catcher called time and went out to the mound to talk to the pitcher, a beach ball bounced onto the field, or a hot dog wrapper twirled around home plate, delaying play …

Was it a grand conspiracy?

Nope, it was the Vinny rule. NOTHING happened on the field until he finished his story.

In one game I was announcing, there were runners at first and second, with no outs. It seemed like a pretty safe time to tell a story, as the end of the inning seemingly a long way off.

On the next pitch after I started the story, a ground ball was hit near the bag at third. The third baseman caught it, stepped on the bag for the first out, threw to second base for the second out, then on to first to complete a triple play. No outs, one pitch, a triple play, the inning was over, and so was my story.

That would NEVER happen to Vinny!

Part of his charm is his great sense of humor. Both of us are left-handed and, occasionally, he called me "The Redhead." He once told me that I was his mother's favorite player, adding, "The fact that we both have red hair and are left-handed has nothing to do with it."

Singers go on stage and entertain an audience for a couple of hours. Vinny went on the air and entertained viewers and listeners for an entire summer. He gave his audience facts about particular players, and overall baseball history. He weaved in stories about the players when they were growing up, or what they did in the minor leagues. In my case, he mentioned a couple of things about me that even I had forgotten.

But beyond baseball, he would talk about how Mother's Day originated, or interesting facts about the Fourth of July. I heard him go into great detail on the history of the American flag. I saw a video of that game and it was so good, I watched it five times.

The audience always got so much more listening to Vinny than just balls, strikes, and the scores of other games. He is the most prepared, creative, and interesting announcer I've ever listened to, always coming up with new ways to entertain his fans.

Back in the early 1960s, the Dodgers had an exhibition game against a college team. All the information Vinny had on the school was only what he got from its athletic department, and that wasn't much. He had the players' height, weight, their stats, and what year they were in at school. How was that going to work? How was Vinny going to fill nine innings without all the usual, wonderful background notes on the players?

He came up with an idea only he could have thought of. He made up his own lineup for the Dodgers' opposing team. Instead of the college players, he substituted Hall of Famers at every position, players like Babe Ruth, Lou Gehrig, Ty Cobb, Honus Wagner, Jimmy Foxx, Walter Johnson, Christy Mathewson, and Cy Young. For the listeners that day, the Dodgers were facing the greatest players in the history of the game.

Vinny never ran out of things to talk about on that broadcast.

I got a couple of hits that day, and I think they were off Cy Young and Christy Mathewson.

One of the sights unique to Dodger Stadium is the taillights leaving the ballpark starting around the seventh inning. In a city where traffic jams pop up on the freeway seemingly at all times of the day and night, fans, many of them with a long drive home and the need to get up early for work the next day, want to beat the traffic out of the stadium. It was also Vinny's fault that they left, because he was so damn good.

They listened to the remainder of the game in their cars on their way home, and fans knew that listening to Vinny was the next best thing to being there. Sometimes, depending on their seat, even better. He made his audience part of the game. He made his listeners feel like they were on the field, in the batter's box, or on the mound. Even when they were in their car.

I once asked Vinny if it was possible to have a perfect game as an announcer.

"I don't know if you can," he said, "because you don't know what is about to happen in the game. You can always go back and say, 'If I knew what was going to take place, I might have been able to set it up a little better.'"

Sorry, Vinny, but I disagree. I've heard you announce thousands of perfect games.

## SAN FRANCISCO

I left the Angels in 1986 after eight seasons as a broadcaster when I was offered the chance to be a lead announcer in the broadcast booth of the Giants, once my most hated rival.

The feeling was mutual. The fans in San Francisco had no fond memories of me, a former Dodger.

Strike one.

I was from Southern California.

Strike two.

And, I was taking over for popular announcer Hank Greenwald, who left because of a contract dispute with KNBR, the Giants' radio station.

Strike three.

So I was walking into a hornets' nest. I was criticized before I said, "Hello, everybody, and welcome to Scottsdale, and the opening game of spring training."

Some nasty things were written about me in the local papers. A close friend, whom I had known since the third grade, was living in the Bay Area. He wrote several nice letters to the editor about me, but they never appeared in the paper. I told him to try writing a nasty letter. He did and — surprise — it appeared in the paper.

Hank patched things up with his old bosses and returned to the booth as my broadcast partner three years later, and I'm so happy he did. Working with Hank was a real pleasure, and I learned a lot from him.

He would always say, "It may not be a good game, but it doesn't have to be a bad broadcast." He was 100 percent right about that. Announcers have to prepare for a bad game — that's right, a bad game — because that's when we earn our money. The exciting or important games move quickly. On those broadcasts, I didn't use most of my notes.

But for the inevitable long or boring games, announcers must have in their back pocket a topic, a story, a date in baseball history, an interesting stat like the last player to have more RBIs than games played in a season (George Brett, 1980, 117 games played, 118 RBIs) ... something to talk about. Fortunately, as an announcer, I had collected almost as many stories over the years as I had during my playing days. And sooner or later, I needed them.

When Hank had to fill air time, he had enough material to write a book. Literally. This was before the advent of the internet, which has brought all the facts and figures an announcer could want within reach of his fingertips. But then, Hank carried around close to 200 pages of historical facts on hitting, pitching, and every date in baseball history. He was always ready, regardless of how long the game lasted.

And like all of us in the broadcast business, Hank worked hard at his job. Most fans think announcers get to the park, go straight to the booth, turn on their microphones, and start talking. In reality, visiting with players and managers before the game to get notes, doing the pregame show, announcing the games, and hosting the postgame results in an eight- to 10-hour day.

Just like with every other team I've been with, I got my share of interesting and funny stories with the Giants.

In a spring training game, Roger Craig, then the team's manager, told Norm Sherry, then the pitching coach, to go out to the mound and take the pitcher out. Sherry, who hadn't been watching the game because he was on another field working with other pitchers, went to the mound, but didn't make the requested change. When he returned to the dugout, Craig, puzzled, said, "I told you to take the pitcher out."

"I know," said Sherry, "but he told me he got this batter out the last time he faced him."

"I know that," said Craig, "but this is the second time he's facing him in this inning."

Before every Sunday home game, the Giants would gather in their dining area after batting practice to play Trivial Pursuit. We called it "The Caveman Quiz" because the questions were read by Don Robinson, a pitcher whose nickname was "The Caveman." Don regularly messed up the questions, and his West Virginia accent complicated things further. Here are some of the memorable questions and answers.

Robinson: Where are the Spice Islands?

Answer: Off Chile.

Robinson: What country borders on the Yukon?

Answers: Canada? Russia? Alaska?

Robinson: All wrong.

Finally, fellow pitcher Mike Krukow grabbed the card from Robinson, and said, "No wonder we can't get it. The question is, What country borders on the Yucatán?"

Robinson: What is the longest nerve in the human body?

Pitcher Craig Lefferts, without hesitation: The optical nerve.

Robinson: Why would you say that?

Lefferts: Because when you pull a hair out of your ass, your eyes water.

## SEATTLE

In 1993, I went to work in the Seattle Mariners broadcast booth alongside Dave Niehaus and Rick Rizzs. Another newcomer to the Mariners that season was the manager, Lou Piniella.

He had been a damn good player who lasted 18 years in the majors, 11 of them with the Yankees. He was fiery, had a temper, and was an intense competitor. He managed much the same way, serving as the skipper of the Yankees and Reds before coming to Seattle.

The Mariners were coming off a 64-98 season. "Look at these players," he told me, pointing out Ken Griffey Jr., Randy Johnson, Edgar Martínez, Tino Martinez, Jay Buhner, and many others. "How in the world did these guys lose 98 games? It makes no sense to me." Lou must

Quirky Dave Niehaus, left, was Ron's broadcast partner for the Seattle Mariners, for whom Ron called games for 14 years.

have said that 20 or 30 times the first two weeks.

With a new training facility under construction in Peoria, Arizona, the Mariners had to play all of their exhibition games that spring on the road. They lost their first nine.

"I said I couldn't understand how they lost 98 games," Lou told Dave Niehaus and me. "After watching them play this spring, I'm trying to figure out how the hell they won 64 games."

Lou realized he had to change the attitude of the players. He could not stand to lose, but many of his players accepted losing too easily.

After the Mariners lost again, dropping their exhibition record to 0-10, the team bus, on its way back to Peoria, drove by a high school where a baseball game was in progress. "Stop here," Lou told the bus driver, then turned to his players, and said, "Let's see if you can beat one of those teams."

Nobody laughed.

When the Mariners finally won their first game, Lou told me, "I was considering putting Champagne in the clubhouse."

Mike Schooler, one of Seattle's relievers from the year before, was quoted as saying, "Piniella puts too much emphasis on winning."

What? That was the attitude Lou had to change. Schooler did not make the team, released before spring training ended.

Lou was determined to change the mindset of the Mariners' organization. He drove the front office a little crazy, asking them to trade this player or sign that player.

But things did change. In his first season at the helm, Seattle finished 82-80, an 18-game improvement over the previous year. In his 10 years as manager, Lou got the Mariners into the postseason four times, but they could never get to the World Series. Three times they lost in the American League Championship Series, twice to the Yankees. The most painful exit was in 2001, losing to New York in the ALCS after winning 116 regular-season games, tying the Cubs for the most in baseball history.

Lou didn't have much patience after losses, and he had even less patience with agents. One night, the Mariners lost a game they were leading until the bullpen gave up four runs in the late innings. The pitcher who gave up two of the runs was the client of an agent who called Lou that night to tell him that his client should be the closer on the team.

Lou's response was short and to the point.

"Your client is closer to going back to the minor leagues," he told the agent, "than he is to becoming the closer on my team."

One night in Toronto, the Blue Jays scored two quick runs early against the Mariners. Lou went to the mound and asked the pitcher if he felt OK. The pitcher said he did.

"Well, I don't," said Lou. "The way you're pitching is making me sick."

He was always complaining that his front office wouldn't get him the players he needed. On many nights, I would go out to dinner with him and some of his coaches. When the waiter would come over, Lou would often say, "Order whatever you want. If the Mariners won't spend any money to get me a left fielder or a pitcher, I'll make them spend the money on our dinner."

We had some characters on those teams. There was a right-handed pitcher who went down after one season to pitch winter ball in Venezuela. When he got there, he bought himself a big, flat-screen TV, but, when the season was over, he left it in Venezuela.

The next spring, he was telling some of his fellow Mariners about winter ball, and mentioned that he had left the new TV down there.

Why? he was asked.

"Because I couldn't use it here at home," he said. "All it played were Spanish stations."

In 2006, I retired at the age of 68. Five years later, I returned to my old job in the Mariners' broadcast booth.

It was the last place I wanted to be, considering the circumstances. I was there because Dave Niehaus was not. My longtime broadcast partner, the man I worked with, laughed with, and shared nearly a decade and a half of great experiences, had died unexpectedly during the off-season in 2010.

I have more stories about Dave than about any of the guys I ever played with. He had a terrible sense of direction, whether it was in search of the elevator after leaving the press box, or in search of a particular restaurant while we were driving down the road. Several times, he set a trash can in the broadcast booth on fire by tossing a lit cigarette into it, and once inadvertently took my microphone, leaving me standing useless in front of the camera — it was like sending me up to the plate without a bat. Dave had an egg timer that he always placed near his microphone to remind him to mention the score when the sand ran out. In all the years I worked with him, I never, ever remember him turning it over.

One day, I picked up Dave at his apartment to drive him to the stadium before a game. I didn't notice until we got to the ballpark that he was wearing two different sandals, one old and one new. When I told him I liked his new style, he responded with a smile, "Thanks, I have another pair just like these at the apartment."

That was Dave. He might leave you shaking your head, but ultimately, you would wind up laughing, never at him, always with him. He was a joy to work with.

Although he might have laughed a lot, he was always serious when it

**Ron almost ran out of fingers to display his championship rings. From left, 1960 AAA Pacific Coast League, 1965 World Series, 1959 World Series, 1973 All-Star, 1963 World Series, 1977 All-Star, 1989 National League (as a Giants announcer).**

came to his work ethic. He was committed to the job. He always wanted to be at the park early so as not to miss anything. Some days we got to the stadium before some of the players. Two or three times, we had to find a security guard to unlock the press box doors so we could get in the booth.

I am so thankful that Dave lived long enough to receive the ultimate honor that can be bestowed on a baseball broadcaster — the Ford C. Frick Award, given to him in 2008 by the Hall of Fame. He richly deserved it — he was a damn good announcer.

It was so painful to be in that booth without him.

I still miss him today.

Finally, at the end of the 2012 season, I retired for good. I had spent 14 years in Seattle, 30 years in broadcasting, and 20 years as a major league player. A nice round total of 50 years in the game I love.

I have been truly blessed.

# 15

## What a Difference
## a Half-Century Makes

S OME ASPECTS OF BASEBALL remain unchanged from a century ago. A player still has to run 90 feet to reach to first base, it's still three strikes and you're out, and crowds still love to boo the umpire. But they don't yell, "Kill the ump!" anymore, so, I guess that's progress.

Some things, however, did change over the half-century I spent in the game. Here are a few:

**Money:** It's the biggest difference in the game.

Walter O'Malley was once asked what he would have had to pay Koufax if he had pitched in the free-agent era. "Sandy and I," said O'Malley with a smile, "would have been partners."

In 1966, Koufax and Don Drysdale refused to report to spring training, holding out for a six-figure salary. That was considered outrageous for a pitcher back then. In his autobiography, "Once a Bum, Always a Dodger," Don wrote, "… asking for $100,000 wasn't like asking for the moon. It was like asking for the moon plus the rest of the solar system."

After a holdout that dragged on through nearly all of spring training, Sandy signed for $125,000, Don for $115,000.

In 2017, Clayton Kershaw was paid $33.6 million for the season, a 26,780 percent increase over Sandy's groundbreaking salary.

When we won the World Series in 1959, Buzzie Bavasi told me that the payroll for the Dodgers' 40-man roster was $850,000. In 2017, the team payroll was just under $186 million. The average major league salary is $4.5 million.

Nobody is losing money. The gross revenues of Major League Baseball are more than $10 billion.

**The Knockdown Pitch:** An accepted part of the game 50 years ago, it is illegal today and that's a good thing.

We usually had one-year contracts, but players today have multi-year deals worth so much that the owners decided it just didn't make any sense to throw at someone's head.

Still, I think it would interesting to see how today's hitters would handle the challenge of knowing a pitcher might flip them on their backs now and then.

I was knocked on my ass many times. I always thought of it as a compliment, because I was doing something that pissed the pitcher off — getting hits and driving in runs.

Back then, it was us against them. With the reserve clause keeping us tied to one team, unless we were traded, we would be together for much, if not all, of our careers. We grew extremely close, so knocking down one of us was like knocking down all of us. And we did respond.

**Hitting Instructors:** We didn't have any.

We just talked among ourselves. I got a lot of great tips from Duke Snider, Carl Furillo, Tommy Davis, Jim Gilliam, and so many others. It was the little suggestions that made us better hitters, and tougher outs. I also talked, whenever possible, to the best hitters in baseball, like Ted Williams and Stan Musial.

I once asked Musial if he did anything different when hitting off left-handed pitchers. He told me to make sure I kept my eyes level. That would allow me to see the ball better. "If someone asks you to line up something with your eyes," he said, "do you tilt your head to one side? No, you keep your eyes level." He was right. It worked.

**The Equipment:** Players get what they need today, whether it's bats, shoes, fielding gloves, or batting gloves.

When I was playing, the Rawlings company gave us two fielding gloves a year, and the shoe companies did the same with their product. If we needed more, we had to personally pay for whatever we got.

**The Ballparks:** Although the clubhouse and all the other facilities in the new stadiums are bigger, the dimensions of the playing fields are smaller, from left center to right center.

The owners and the fans like the home runs because it makes the games more entertaining.

**Game Strategy:** There are a lot more home runs hit today, a lot more strikeouts, and fewer sacrifice bunts.

They also don't hit-and-run as much, because strikeouts leave the runner vulnerable to being thrown out.

Players are bigger and stronger, and their approach to hitting is different. It's about the home runs, not the batting average. More and more players, like the Dodgers' Justin Turner and Cody Bellinger, and the Cubs' Kris Bryant, use an uppercut swing to try to hit the ball in the air and, ideally, out of the park.

If I played today, I would probably try to hit more home runs too, but it is difficult for me to call a player a great hitter if he strikes out 150 or 200 times a year. Great hitters don't do that.

Some of the all-time great power hitters proved that swinging for the fences doesn't have to mean all or nothing:

- Hank Aaron: 22 seasons, 755 home runs, .305 career batting average, 60.1 average strikeouts per season
- Babe Ruth: 22 seasons, 714 HRs, .342, 60.5 average Ks
- Willie Mays: 22 seasons, 660 HRs, .302, 69.4 average Ks
- Frank Robinson: 21 seasons, 586 HRs, .294, average 73 Ks
- Ted Williams: 19 seasons, 521 HRs, .344, 37.3 average Ks
- Stan Musial: 22 seasons, 425 HRs, .331, 31.6 average Ks
- Joe DiMaggio: 13 seasons, 361 HRs, .325, 28.4 average Ks.

Every player has slumps. It was easy to lose perspective when I was grinding away at the plate, trying to find my way out of a downward spiral.

So, before the next game, I stepped back to appreciate how lucky I was. I walked out to the outfield, turned around, looked at the 50,000 people in the seats, and reminded myself that slump or no slump, so many of those fans would love to be standing where I was, wearing my uniform.

My worst day in a baseball uniform was better than the best day I could have had in any other career.

# A Life in the Golden Era
# of Baseball

## Early Innings: 1938-1958

**1938** — Ronald Ray Fairly is born July 12, in Macon, Georgia. In October, the family — dad Carl, mom Marjorie, and older brother Rusty — moves to Southern California. Carl, a minor league baseball player, teaches Ron and Rusty about sports.

**1953-56** — Ron attends Long Beach Jordan High School. A star athlete, he's recruited for the UCLA basketball team by John Wooden. But baseball is his game, overcoming an early disappointment with an assignment to a youth league team sponsored by Miriam's Beauty Bar. "I hated that jersey," he says.

**1957-58** —Ron commits to playing baseball at USC, where Rod Dedeaux is in the early stages of his legendary career as the Trojans' baseball coach. In spring of 1958, Ron plays a practice game with the Trojans in the Los Angeles Memorial Coliseum, where, a few weeks later, the Dodgers play their first game in Los Angeles after moving west from Brooklyn, New York. Along with 78,672 other fans, Ron is there for the Dodgers Opening Day, April 18, 1958. Two months later, USC, with sophomore Ron Fairly as one of its stars, wins the College World Series. That summer, Ron decides to turn pro.

## Middle Innings: 1958-1969

**1958** — Ron rejects a $100,000 offer from the White Sox, and signs with the Dodgers for $75,000 on June 24. Soon, he's off to the minor leagues. By September, when the big league clubs call up more players at season's end, Ron is back at the Coliseum — on the roster for the hometown team he watched start the season in that stadium five months earlier.

**1959** — After spring training, Ron expects to get a minor league assignment, but he makes the Dodgers roster for Opening Day. He plays in 118 games and hits .238 in a season that ends with the Dodgers playing in the World Series the year

**1966** — Another full season for Ron and another World Series, but this time, the outcome is different. The Orioles sweep the Dodgers, who manage to score only two runs in the entire series.

**1969** — After more than 10 years with the Dodgers, Ron is traded. On June 11, he is sent to the Montreal Expos for Manny Mota and Maury Wills. It's a new country and a new climate, requiring a new attitude. He adjusts.

## Late Innings: 1969-1979

**1971-73** — Ron plays in more than 140 games in each year. He makes his first All-Star team in 1973.

**1974-76** — Ron is traded to the Cardi-nals, and starts the 1975 season in St. Louis. He hits .301 and plays through

after Ron played in the College World Series. As did the Trojans, the Dodgers win their series, in seven games over the Chicago White Sox. It is the first of four World Series in which Ron will play. He is 21.

**1960-65** — Ron plays in only 14 games with the Dodgers in 1960. After six months of military service in the winter of

1959-60, he was back in the minors before being called back up late in the season. But in 1961, he hits a career-high .322, and has a career-best .522 slugging percentage. He is now an estab-lished Dodgers star. In 1963, the team makes it back to the World Series and faces the formidable and hated Yankees, who had been in 13 of the previous 16 World Series, and

won 10 of them. Not this time. The Dodgers win, and they sweep the series. Ron calls it "the most important moment in Dodgers history."

**1965** — Ron plays in 158 games, and the Dodgers win another World Series. They beat the Twins in seven games, with Sandy Koufax winning the clincher and striking out 10 in the process.

two productive seasons in St. Louis, challenging the mound territorialism of his teammate, Bob Gibson.

**1976-77** — Ron is purchased by the Oakland A's, and finds owner Charlie Finley to be as cheap as his reputation promises. By 1977, Ron is back in Canada, this time with the Toronto Blue Jays, where, at 39, he has a good enough season to make his second All-Star team.

**1978** — Ron comes back home to California and a $125,000 contract with the Angels. He hits his last major league home run on Sept. 12, the date on which he hit his first, in 1958. He plays his last major league game on Sept. 23. In spring 1979, owner Gene Autry offers Ron a broadcast job. He takes it, trading the batter's box for the broadcast booth.

## Extra Innings: 1979-2012

**1979-86** — Ron broadcasts for the Angels, including spring training games in Palm Springs, where comedian Phil Harris was known to visit the booth and disrupt the play-calling with goofy tales of celebrities behaving badly. In 1986, Ron moves north, into the broadcast booth of the Dodgers' longtime rivals, the San Francisco Giants.

**1986-2012** — At first, Ron recalls, "They hated me. I was a Dodger." Eventually fans warmed to him, and he learns valuable lessons from Giants broadcaster Hank Greenwald that he takes to Seattle in 1993. His announcing partner is Dave Niehaus, whom he describes as "a joy to work with," until 2006, when Ron retires. Five years later, he unretires to fill the gaping broadcast void when Niehaus dies. Ron says goodbye to baseball for good at the end of the 2012 season in Seattle.

— *Bill Dwyre,*
*Back Story Publishing*

# Fairly at the Plate

Key to abbreviations: LG (league), G (games), AB (at bats), R (runs), H (hits), TB (total bases), 2B (doubles), 3B (triples), HR (home runs), RBI (runs batted in), BB (bases on balls), IBB (intentional bases on balls), SO (strikeouts), SB (stolen bases), CS (caught stealing), AVG (batting average), OBP (on base percentage), SLG. (slugging percentage), OPS (on-base plus slugging percentage).

| Year | Team | LG | G | AB | R | H | TB | 2B | 3B | HR |
|------|------|-----|------|------|-----|------|------|-----|-----|-----|
| 1958 | LA | NL | 15 | 53 | 6 | 15 | 22 | 1 | 0 | 2 |
| 1959 | LA | NL | 118 | 244 | 27 | 58 | 84 | 12 | 1 | 4 |
| 1960 | LA | NL | 14 | 37 | 6 | 4 | 13 | 0 | 3 | 1 |
| 1961 | LA | NL | 111 | 245 | 42 | 79 | 128 | 15 | 2 | 10 |
| 1962 | LA | NL | 147 | 460 | 80 | 128 | 199 | 15 | 7 | 14 |
| 1963 | LA | NL | 152 | 490 | 62 | 133 | 190 | 21 | 0 | 12 |
| 1964 | LA | NL | 150 | 454 | 62 | 116 | 175 | 19 | 5 | 10 |
| 1965 | LA | NL | 158 | 555 | 73 | 152 | 209 | 28 | 1 | 9 |
| 1966 | LA | NL | 117 | 351 | 53 | 101 | 163 | 20 | 0 | 14 |
| 1967 | LA | NL | 153 | 486 | 45 | 107 | 156 | 19 | 0 | 10 |
| 1968 | LA | NL | 141 | 441 | 32 | 103 | 132 | 15 | 1 | 4 |
| 1969 | LA | NL | 30 | 64 | 3 | 14 | 21 | 3 | 2 | 0 |
| 1969 | MON | NL | 70 | 253 | 35 | 73 | 130 | 13 | 4 | 12 |
| 1969 [-] | 2 teams | - | 100 | 317 | 38 | 87 | 151 | 16 | 6 | 12 |
| 1970 | MON | NL | 119 | 385 | 54 | 111 | 175 | 19 | 0 | 15 |
| 1971 | MON | NL | 146 | 447 | 58 | 115 | 177 | 23 | 0 | 13 |
| 1972 | MON | NL | 140 | 446 | 51 | 124 | 192 | 15 | 1 | 17 |
| 1973 | MON | NL | 142 | 413 | 70 | 123 | 189 | 13 | 1 | 17 |
| 1974 | MON | NL | 101 | 282 | 35 | 69 | 116 | 9 | 1 | 12 |
| 1975 | STL | NL | 107 | 229 | 32 | 69 | 107 | 13 | 2 | 7 |
| 1976 | OAK | AL | 15 | 46 | 9 | 11 | 21 | 1 | 0 | 3 |
| 1976 | STL | NL | 73 | 110 | 13 | 29 | 33 | 4 | 0 | 0 |
| 1976 [-] | 2 teams | - | 88 | 156 | 22 | 40 | 54 | 5 | 0 | 3 |
| 1977 | TOR | AL | 132 | 458 | 60 | 128 | 213 | 24 | 2 | 19 |
| 1978 | CAL | AL | 91 | 235 | 23 | 51 | 86 | 5 | 0 | 10 |
| MLB Career- | | | 2442 | 7184 | 931 | 1913 | 2931 | 307 | 33 | 215 |

| RBI | BB | IBB | SO | SB | CS | AVG | OBP | SLG | OPS |
|---|---|---|---|---|---|---|---|---|---|
| 8 | 6 | 0 | 7 | 0 | 0 | .283 | .350 | .415 | .765 |
| 23 | 31 | 2 | 29 | 0 | 4 | .238 | .324 | .344 | .668 |
| 3 | 7 | 0 | 12 | 0 | 0 | .108 | .250 | .351 | .601 |
| 48 | 48 | 0 | 22 | 0 | 0 | .322 | .434 | .522 | .956 |
| 71 | 75 | 6 | 59 | 1 | 1 | .278 | .379 | .433 | .811 |
| 77 | 58 | 7 | 69 | 5 | 2 | .271 | .347 | .388 | .735 |
| 74 | 65 | 6 | 59 | 4 | 0 | .256 | .349 | .385 | .734 |
| 70 | 76 | 11 | 72 | 2 | 0 | .274 | .361 | .377 | .738 |
| 61 | 52 | 4 | 38 | 3 | 2 | .288 | .380 | .464 | .844 |
| 55 | 54 | 9 | 51 | 1 | 4 | .220 | .295 | .321 | .616 |
| 43 | 41 | 10 | 61 | 0 | 2 | .234 | .301 | .299 | .600 |
| 8 | 9 | 1 | 6 | 0 | 0 | .219 | .315 | .328 | .643 |
| 39 | 28 | 2 | 22 | 1 | 0 | .289 | .358 | .514 | .872 |
| 47 | 37 | 3 | 28 | 1 | 0 | .274 | .349 | .476 | .826 |
| 61 | 72 | 9 | 64 | 10 | 2 | .288 | .402 | .455 | .857 |
| 71 | 81 | 10 | 65 | 1 | 3 | .257 | .373 | .396 | .769 |
| 68 | 46 | 7 | 45 | 3 | 4 | .278 | .348 | .430 | .779 |
| 49 | 86 | 11 | 33 | 2 | 2 | .298 | .422 | .458 | .880 |
| 43 | 57 | 6 | 28 | 2 | 1 | .245 | .372 | .411 | .784 |
| 37 | 45 | 9 | 22 | 0 | 1 | .301 | .421 | .467 | .888 |
| 10 | 9 | 3 | 12 | 0 | 0 | .239 | .364 | .457 | .820 |
| 21 | 23 | 3 | 12 | 0 | 0 | .264 | .385 | .300 | .685 |
| 31 | 32 | 6 | 24 | 0 | 0 | .256 | .379 | .346 | .725 |
| 64 | 58 | 11 | 58 | 0 | 4 | .279 | .362 | .465 | .827 |
| 40 | 25 | 2 | 31 | 0 | 1 | .217 | .289 | .366 | .655 |
| 1044 | 1052 | 129 | 877 | 35 | 33 | .266 | .360 | .408 | .768 |

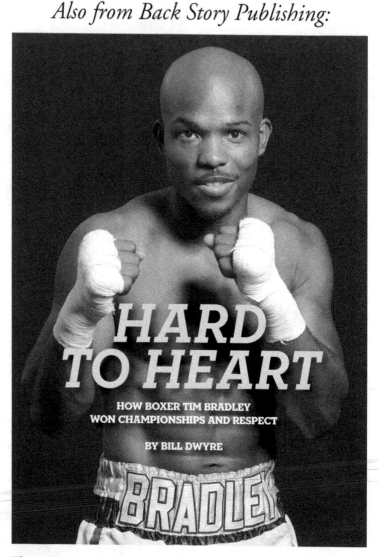

CPSIA information can be obtained
at www.ICGtesting.com
Printed in the USA
LVHW03s0303150818
587029LV00007B/167/P

9 780999 396728